Discerning
God's Will

Discerning God's Will

Ben Campbell Johnson

Westminster/John Knox Press
Louisville, Kentucky

Book design by Polebridge Press

First edition

Published by Westminster/John Knox Press
Louisville, Kentucky

PRINTED IN THE UNITED STATES OF AMERICA
9 8 7 6 5 4 3 2 1

Library of Congress Cataloging-in-Publication Data

Johnson, Ben Campbell.
    Discerning God's will / Ben Campbell Johnson. — 1st ed.
        p.   cm.
    Includes bibliographical references.
    ISBN 0-664-25146-3

    1. God—Will.   2. Discernment of spirits.   3. Christian
life—1960–   I. Title.
BV4501.2.J537 1990
248.4—dc20   90-33003
                                                            CIP

Contents

The L*ORD* *will fulfil*
   his purpose for me;
thy steadfast love, O L*ORD*,
   endures for ever.
Do not forsake the work
   of thy hands.
                         Psalm 138:8

Preface

For the past twelve years I have experienced a deepening interest in God. I could call this a love for God, but the word "love" has become so washed out that it does not communicate what I have felt. My interest has become a passion burning within me and has directed me on my journey.

In two previous books, *To Will God's Will* and *To Pray God's Will,* I have described life as a journey. In them I suggested certain spiritual disciplines to deepen the sense of God on the journey.

I intend here to address the issue of discernment, the discernment of the meaning of our lives. I begin with the assumption that all of us have a deep, if not controlling, desire for meaning. We want our lives to count for something.

In the chapters that follow, I show how the hunger for meaning is a disguised hunger for the will of God, a reality that has been made visible in Jesus Christ. Christ stands as the norm for discerning God's will.

With Christ as the norm, I explore our creation in the image of God, our intuition, our imagination, our memory, and our will to obedience as tools for discernment. Although never absolute in the data they provide, these faculties of the soul offer our only means for the knowledge of God.

After laying out these various faculties of discernment, I deal with the thorniest problem of all in the search for meaning: the problem of evil. When radical evil expresses itself—through accidents, calamities, or death—it often destroys whatever meaning we have been able to find. How do we then begin again? How do we find God in and through our suffering? Some readers may be in such darkness and pain through personal loss that they may need to begin with chapter 9 on the issue of evil and the exercise for chapter 9 in Appendix A, which will help them to appropriate the insights of the chapter.

The final chapter places the practice of corporate discernment in the life and work of the congregation. In this discerning community, we discover the will of God both for our own lives and for our mission to the world. I set forth a vision of the church as a community of discernment, although I do not know just how that would look in a mainline congregation. But some groups may be willing to explore ways of becoming a community of discernment.

Each chapter has a parallel exercise in Appendix A. These exercises offer a way of appropriating the insights of the chapters. I hope that at some time you will use them as guidelines for journaling. If you are unfamiliar with the spiritual discipline of journaling, see Appendix A, pages 95–107, of *To Will God's Will.*

Finally, my hopes for this investigation of discernment: I hope some person confused about the meaning of his or her life will find in these chapters suggestions that will be of help in picking up the trail of meaning once again. I hope this effort will deepen the sense of God in all our churches and offer help in discerning the divine purpose for our mission in history. And I hope you, the reader, take as much delight in reading these words as I have taken in writing them.

Epiphany, 1990

One

The Search for Meaning

What is the meaning of my life?

That question, in one form or another, has always been a matter of concern for me. Its urgency deepened for me when, at an early age, I realized that one day I would die.

I don't know why that awareness came to me when it did, but I vividly recall the moment. I was nine years old, visiting my uncle John B. Johnson's home. While I was crossing the highway that separated the barn from the house, the thought broke into my consciousness: One day I will die.

What causes such a thought? Where did it come from? Why did it occur to me at that particular moment? These questions are difficult to answer.

Perhaps it was because I had often heard the story of my great-grandfather's being fatally injured by an automobile while crossing that very highway. Maybe I was at an age to exercise the uniquely human capacity to anticipate the future, and thus my own death. Or could this awareness have been a gift from God?

I don't know which of these speculations is right—maybe all or none. Regardless of why the thought came, one thing I know: It did come, and it has caused me to feel the value of life.

It has given me urgency in my quest for the meaning of my one and only life.

As someone said, "Something that is yours forever is never precious." Is not this one reason why all our lives are precious? Does not their brevity and boundedness intensify our search for meaning? I'm certain my own awareness of finitude has fueled my sense of urgency in finding the meaning of my life. So I have asked the question of meaning in a dozen ways and in as many contexts.

The question of my life's meaning, which received so much energy from the awareness of my death when I was just nine years old, surfaced again in late adolescence, when I asked, "What am I to do with my life?" but the urgency of the question subsided while I prepared for ministry.

Then, during the third decade of my life, the question came once more, this time with a nagging, fearful persistency. It marked my memory with several clear turning points.

Sometimes after my twenty-fifth year I thought again about the meaning of my life. In this period I had a persistent fear that I might reach the end of my life and all my efforts would have come to naught. If that were the case, I might just as well never have been. Sometimes the horror of living to no end disturbed me so deeply that I had trouble sleeping.

As I neared my thirtieth year, the struggle became more intense. For years I had been "approaching" life; now I was "there." I don't know why the thirtieth year had such an effect, but I felt like a three-year-old racehorse at Churchill Downs on Derby day. "I am in the starting gate, the bell is about to sound, and I will begin the 'run for the roses'; I run either now or never. One race, one chance for my life."

This pressure became most intense while I was pastoring a small church in Phenix City, Alabama. At the time I was weighing the alternatives of going back to school to study for a Ph.D. in religion or remaining in pastoral ministry. With my mind tossing like a sailboat in the ocean, a pastor friend asked me a mind-settling question. "If you could be pastor of the largest, most influential church in this state, would that fulfill your life dream?"

That question thrust me twenty-five years into the future. As I mentally placed myself in the most significant pulpit in the state, nothing within me responded to the vision. In a strange way, projecting myself into the future forced the decision. I would resign from the church, enroll in graduate school, and pursue a doctorate.

I made that choice without having been accepted in graduate school and with no money for tuition, no job, and no house to move into. Do not think the decision was anxiety-free. So deep were my questions and so troublesome my fears that I spent one entire night in the church sanctuary praying for guidance and assurance. I read the scriptures and listened for God through the night. As dawn neared, a few words came to me, words spoken to Abram: "Go from your country and your kindred and your father's house to the land that I will show you .... So Abram went, as the LORD had told him" (Gen. 12:1, 4).

These words strengthened my conviction to return to school and helped me entrust my future to God. I went out not knowing where the path would lead. Yet I believed I was compelled by God to follow it. In all the years that have passed, I have never doubted that I made the right decision. Both when making that decision and afterward I have felt deeply that I had only one life and one opportunity to live it; I had to discover the possibility my life held.

When I got within ten years of retirement, I felt once again the urgency of the question of my life's meaning. For a decade or so, I had been counting time not in terms of age but in terms of how much longer I had to live. I saw clearly that I had another ten or fifteen years, at most, to be productive. Time was moving fast. Perhaps in my formative years I could afford to make mistakes and take detours, but not now. My time was too brief, my sense of urgency too great, and my life too precious to squander.

Out of this concern for the future I felt a call to the desert, a call to pray about the remainder of my life. So, at age fifty-five, I went to New Mexico, secluded myself in a tiny monastery, and for two weeks made the remaining years of my life a matter of concentrated prayer and disciplined imagination.

Each day I anticipated the future with a sense that "it is too late in life for trivia." I imagined myself living until the day of my death, hoping the images that came to me contained hints about the meaning of my life.

For most of my days on earth, therefore, I have been concerned with the meaning of my life. Am I odd? Is this experience strange? Does not every person, at strategic moments, struggle with this same question?

The Human Hunger for Meaning

Surely I am not alone in this hunger for meaning; others, too, have asked this question with the same or greater passion. But this very pursuit raises another important question: What do we mean by "meaning"? "Meaning," like "pleasure," is a slippery term.

For example, how do you define the word "pleasure"? A woman attends the symphony and reports that she felt a deep sense of pleasure while listening to the music of Mozart. What does she mean, good feelings? A sense of identification with the music? An existential moment of unity with a reality beyond the sounds of the musical instruments? These definitions fail to communicate the true significance of "pleasure."

Definitions of "meaning" also leave us with a list of similar questions. Dictionaries are of little help. They speak of something "in the mind, view, or contemplation as a settled aim or purpose," something intended or implied. These words fail to reach into the depths of the human psyche and evoke an image that applies to one's whole life.

If "meaning" cannot be reduced to a short dictionary definition, perhaps it can be understood by viewing its different facets. Like a diamond, it sends light in many directions. Perhaps an impressionistic description of "meaning" will provide help.

"Meaning" hints of intention, and exists in the mind as a settled aim or goal. What is intended? Intention points toward the future; an intended deed, achievement, or result always lies in the future. Does not the meaning of life point toward a positive future?

But a positive vision of the future does not appear out of nowhere. The vision receives images from the past, in which it is grounded. "Meaning," therefore, relates to a past in which the soul has experienced a satisfaction or fulfillment that it hopes to continue and enlarge. Or it relates to a past that contains a painful circumstance from which the soul envisions release.

Meaning also depends on the continuity of events in a person's life. Meaning cannot be sustained by flashes that occur like beams from a rotating beacon. Meaning requires continuity and relatedness to connect the events of our lives. If meaning did not have continuity, we would be like drowning swimmers surfacing each two or three minutes for a gulp of air.

But we must not think of meaning as a static possession to receive, protect, and hold. It is the experience of the moment; it is a dynamic awareness in the "now" that is built on the memory of the past in anticipation of a desired future. Because every "now" is a vanishing point, meaning is always arriving and leaving; therefore, it occurs in the present moment.

Because meaning occurs in the present, achieving it requires a place—a personal, social environment. Meaning never occurs in a vacuum, but only in our awareness as we find ourselves woven into relationships in and through which meaning evolves.

My own experience, to which I have already referred, will perhaps illustrate the meaning of "meaning." At age thirty I was poised to embark on an uncharted future that held the meaning of my life; I did not see that future clearly, but I had hungered to do or be something that would count in the world. I envisioned a future of research in spiritual renewal and a daring commitment of my life.

My intention for the future had connections with my past. I had for all of my Christian life been concerned with introducing others to a personal Christ; I had experimented with various ways of achieving this goal; for instance, through small groups and lay witness. My future was likely to be conditioned by this central concern and by new methods for realizing it. Meaning, for me, had continuity with my past values and experiences and the unknown future that challenged me.

The matrix for the birth of this new sense of meaning was a particular church that had experienced a burst of growth in members, buildings, and budget. I had ministered there for five years. Concurrent with these external changes, I had myself experienced a new awareness of Christ through prayer. My age (I was nearing thirty) made the question of meaning particularly acute.

Though I felt deeply about the call of God in my life, this call could not be reduced to a "thing" that I controlled. The identification with Abram gave me conviction enough to leave my place of ministry and start the journey for the unknown country. Again and again God renewed and expanded this conviction. Meaning in some sense is always a quest, a journey, a goal beyond us.

Today I have a different perspective. In my mid-fifties, I know how the story came out. At thirty the future was vision, and hope propelled me onward. Now, I look back at the risk involved, the experiences that ensued, and how these decisions contain the meaning of my one and only life, a meaning that I carry in a narrative.

Whatever meaning we have in our lives may be unearthed in our narratives. The stories of our lives created from our interpretation of the things that have happened to us always carry our life meaning. In contrast with meaning stand the disillusionment and despair that we have in our lives. Despair occurs in a variety of ways—through the loss of a future, the severance of the past, the sacrifice of place, and experiences that do not match our expectations. All these experiences undermine the unity of our life story.

The search for meaning for me has also led through the valley of disillusionment and despair. I followed the "Abram call" to Atlanta and to graduate school. The vague visions I had for the lay witness ministry became realities, and the demands for leadership grew over the next ten years. Then my life was shattered. At age forty I went through a divorce. During all the years of pain, counseling, and renewing covenants, I kept hoping for resolution, but I was not able to put my marriage back together, even with more than ten years of counseling.

Divorce feels like a public failure. With this failure I experienced loss. The future appeared bleak; I saw no role for myself; life seemed to stop.

For the creativity and achievements of the past, I felt grateful, but I seemed to be on a boat drifting away from all that I had valued and that had given life significance.

My life had been like a rose, opening and providing one surprise after another, but then the blooming stopped and all the petals, once so beautiful, began one by one to wither and fall off. Life lost its beauty and sweetness.

The chamber of my soul, where meaning once had dwelt, seemed empty. Once God had spoken, and I had followed with risk and hope. Once I had a future, but now all meaning evaporated. Once I had a place; I was connected to church, to friends, to a role in the work of God. The lines that connected me had been severed, and my life was adrift.

My life story suddenly had reached an unexpected chapter. Divorce did not fit the pattern; it stood over against all that I had hoped for and believed in.

Out of the ashes of despair and failure I had to ask again, "What is the meaning of my life?" Crises like this eclipse meaning, and the question must be asked again.

Some Aspects of the Search

Even when our lives seem devoid of meaning, we find ourselves with instincts and drives that clamor for satisfaction and fulfillment. We long to live and not die; we hunger to belong to significant persons and groups; we need to be valued by others. Are these hungers of the soul not disguised longings for the meaning of our lives?

This hunger for meaning grasps the soul as the profound question of human existence. In the power of self-transcendence, each person asks the question of origin: "Where did I come from?" The question of identity: "Who am I?" The question of purpose: "Why am I here?" And the question of destiny: "Where am I going?" Each question is but a facet of the larger, all-pervasive question of meaning, the purpose of our one and only life.

Human need, separated from satisfaction, and human

questions waiting for slow-emerging answers illustrate the consequences of human estrangement. The situation is compounded by the fact that we do not have the power to cross the chasm that separates us from fulfillment of our ultimate needs and answers to our ultimate questions. We are left to struggle with our needs and speculate about answers to our questions. As a consequence, we human beings seek satisfaction in ways that do not last; we substitute the temporal for the eternal.

Too often we lose the meaning of our lives because we have attached our hope to something or someone who cannot sustain the burden. This mistaken hope opens the issue of ultimate meaning, of that which has the power to give meaning to life and sustain us through disillusionment and despair.

Ultimate Meaning: The Will of God

In my search for meaning, I have come to the unalterable conviction that the will of God offers the final ground, the ultimate power that alone can sustain the meaning of our lives. Every facet of meaning finds fulfillment in the will of God. The will of God promises meaning because it always has dimension in the present. We do the will of God in the present. Only by having intention toward the future and repenting of the past can we deal with God's will. But God's will is always done in the present.

The will of God encompasses the past that we have either violated, fulfilled, or ignored.

The will of God has implications for the future: "What am I to do with my life?"

The will of God is dynamic, not a frozen plan or an unalterable blueprint. It offers meaning in the changes but retains constancy. It remains the same, while coming to us with fresh revelations of the divine intention.

The will of God offers us a place to be—not a physical place, but a psychosocial, spiritual space for intimacy with God.

Thus the will of God meets all our criteria for meaning— the will of God embraces the present, the past that flows into the present, and the future it anticipates, movements made continuous in the memory of God. The will of God includes all the values of life—past, present, and future. Can we not conclude that the ultimate meaning of a person's life is to discern the will of God and to do it? To actualize it in concrete choices?

Although this vision focuses on the search for meaning in a person's life (and this book is written for people as individuals), the principles certainly reach beyond personal need and fulfillment. The will of God operates in social groups, churches, and nations. The final fulfillment of the will of God issues forth in the historical expression of the kingdom of God. While we search for our individual meaning, we should always keep it in the larger perspective.

Distortions of Meaning

I have laid out in some detail my own search for meaning, a search that is finally a search for the will of God. I have also indicated that all of us search for the ultimate meaning of life. Even a cursory examination of human history reveals that human desires focus on pleasures, positions, and possessions as substitutes for God's will. These desires, although not wrong in themselves, turn into "false loves" that do not provide lasting satisfaction to the quest for meaning.

For instance, we seek to survive at the material level. We hunger for food, but food does not satisfy. We build a larger house, or a second home at the beach, and still feel haunted by emptiness because we do not have a place.

We search for security against the threats of life: our doors have locks, our homes have alarm systems, our silver has special markings. We insure our valuables; we lock our money in vaults. But none of this provides ultimate security.

We want to belong, to feel accepted just as we are, to be part of the social structure. We are blind seekers. We choose class. We seek to join the "in" group. Requirements for this group vary with the generations: having the right address, owning a BMW or a Mercedes, belonging to the right country club, wearing brand-name clothes, jetting about the world to exotic vacation spots. All these efforts unmask our desire to belong.

In a similar manner, our ego identity becomes diffused. Too often we look to the signals that others send us, hoping to receive our identity from them; we depend on significant others to convey to us a sense of worth. This stance enables a person to avoid the treacherous inward journey but never leads to a satisfactory identity.

These examples show the myriad ways we invest temporal relations, achievements, and wealth with ultimate significance. Such are the consequences of attaching the meaning of our lives to those things that cannot bear the weight of ultimate meaning.

I recall my own efforts to find the meaning of my life in these false objects. As an adolescent, I believed that if I had the symbols of American success I would like myself and feel confident of my worth. I dreamed of achievements that would cause others to think highly of me. Yet, when those achievements were mine, the affirmations of others did not give meaning to my life.

Though some persons may learn from the failure of others, most of us must discover the hollowness of these temporal fulfillments through our own experience. It seems that our discernment must be sharpened by failed gods in order for us to see more clearly the true God.

The search for a lasting meaning for our lives is like groping through the darkness. Driven by instinct, we try one pathway and then another, seeking the treasure buried in the field. And occasionally into this darkened world of illusion comes a momentary flash of the divine will: it shocks the soul, lays claim on the deluded self, provides a fleeting glimpse of the ultimate. The vision exerts a powerful attraction, an enticement akin to seduction. It liberates the will from its bondage to a deceived freedom. In that moment of illumination, the false attachments appear as vanity and sham; the "true light" has shined.

Do you not see how our confused situation in life necessitates discernment? Deep within us lie desires for security, belonging, and worth, desires pronounced good by God. But innumerable substitutions, perversions, and distortions of fulfillment lure these desires. Blindly, in the grasp of temptation and the lust for immediate fulfillment, we choose transient fulfillments. Does not this situation underline the importance of discernment? Discernment means the ability or capacity to distinguish between preliminary and ultimate means of fulfillment.

Our ultimate fulfillment is in the will of God. In God, who accepts us without reservation, we experience the ultimate belonging, and God's affirmation that we are sons and daughters bestows ultimate worth. Although we may know that being in the will of God meets our deepest needs and answers, our profoundest questions, these broad affirmations of grace and faith find concrete expressions in the daily routine of our lives, as we embrace specific manifestations of the will of God. Even when we have chosen the will of God as the fulfillment of our lives, this blanket choice does not give us supernatural vision to perceive that will instinctively. Again, we see the importance of discernment, which is to view the substance of our lives through the lenses of faith so that we may recognize God's will.

An Image of the Will of God

The human search for meaning is another way of describing the quest for God's will; the hunger for meaning, like an instinct in the psyche, drives us unconsciously long before it becomes a deliberate choice. By living without deliberate choice, we have settled for substitute fulfillments. This state of confusion helps us recognize the crucial role of discernment.

Just what do we mean when we say "the will of God"? Is the will of God like a blueprint detailing foundation, superstructure, and roof? Is it a completed plan that only requires following? Is the will of God a principled effort to be faithful? Is the will of God foreordained, a fate that occurs without human cooperation? Or is the will of God continuously being formed in an open, flexible universe by human freedom, leaving the ultimate outcome in question?

Is the family a model for describing the will of God? Can it be compared to a relation, a sovereign intention that manifests itself to persons as to sons and daughters? Compare it to a mother's relationship to her daughter. The mother teaches her daughter basic rules, shares with her the family tradition, and makes known to her the core vision shared by the family. But the mother grants her daughter freedom to shape her own identity, fulfill her needs, express her talents, and find her vocation in the context of family values. The mother rejoices in her daughter's creativity and celebrates her uniqueness. If she lacks wisdom or proper discernment, the daughter may fail, but the mother has new options for her, new approaches, and a new beginning.

Does not the family image provide an adequate model for God's will? God has written on our souls the divine intention, with watchfulness has nurtured it, bringing it to consciousness. On occasion God has disciplined our lives in order to sharpen our awareness. God gave us a community in which to test our perceptions; when our choices were poor, God supported us through our failures. Is this not the mode of God's will?

If we think of the will of God like the desire of the father and mother for their family, the manner of guidance seems obvious. The child seeks a role model. Do we not have Christ, the embodiment of the will of God, the will of God made flesh?

The child looks to the family tradition—the images, values, and ways of being that the family has accumulated through the years. The child immerses himself or herself in the family's culture. Do we not have a tradition within the church to which we may turn for guidance?

With regard to the compelling intuitions that spring up inside, are these not indicative of God's intuition? Do we not have a conviction about right and truth? As we exercise this faculty, does it not create within us a convictional base?

The son looks to the designer of his personal history over the years, and the pieces of his life begin to form a pattern. He can begin to anticipate the shape of the future. His life becomes like a jigsaw puzzle in which most of the pieces have been placed. Do we not have also the creative imagination to "see" our future with God?

The idea of the will of God being a relationship in the family makes a place for all the faculties of the soul, and it also provides a vision of forgiveness and renewal in the face of failure. For these reasons it offers a positive model for thinking about the nature of God's will in our lives.

In the foregoing discussion I have suggested that basic to all human beings is a quest for the meaning of our lives. I have further identified meaning with the will of God, showing that nothing short of the will of God provides ultimate meaning. But how do we discern the will of God? Why is it so difficult to know what that will is, in particular situations? As a partial context for the issues of discernment, we turn to an exploration of these questions.

Two

The Will of God

In a thousand ways throughout life, we unconsciously inquire into the will of God. "Should I marry? Should I attend this particular school? In what vocation should I engage?" Who has not felt an "ought" or a duty? Perhaps these experiences illustrate the presence of the search for meaning without ever naming the will of God.

But there are also conscious inquiries that the devout soul makes. The questions become more specific: "Is this the will of God for me? How do I discern the will of God?"

In addition to the unconscious and conscious searching for the will of God, experienced souls search for the right forms of obedience. These people know the terrible freedom, the radical freedom of choosing the shape of obedience to God's will, at once a delight and a heavy responsibility.

If "thy will be done on earth as it is in heaven" holds such importance for God, and if the human search for meaning is ultimately the search for God's will, why is the discernment of God's will so difficult? Why does it seem so risky? The answer to these questions arises out of our basic belief structure—the nature of the God-human relationship.

Perhaps the question of a woman I'll call Joane Welke will

22

enable us to get into the crucial issues of discerning the will of God in a particular life situation. Our meeting was to me a strange coincidence. On the first morning of a retreat I was conducting for a church in New York City, I made my way to the lobby. I engaged in conversation with several of the participants who were waiting for the doors to the dining room to be opened for breakfast. When the crowd eagerly dispersed for the meal, I asked the woman standing next to me if she would mind if we sat together.

As soon as we were seated, Joane began talking. Maybe my being the leader lowered her resistance and invited frank confession. I quickly gathered that she had much to tell and had found few ears to listen to her story. She related how she had been reared in New York City by alcoholic parents. Her early church involvement had been modest.

She had married in her early twenties; her husband attended graduate school in North Carolina, an experience of which she had no fond memories. After moving back to the Northeast, she and her husband divorced, a traumatic event that had left her with severe emotional wounds.

During the readjustment period she resigned from a well-paying management job to seek another vocation that offered greater personal fulfillment. Some of her comments led me to believe that her life was being lived in the fast lane.

Having laid out her life before me, she turned abruptly, looked me in the eye, and asked, "How do I find the will of God for my life?" The hunger had been present for years, but now she was naming the urge within: the will of God.

How does one answer such a direct and desperate question? I felt that we needed to have more conversation; I wanted to retreat to some well-tested counseling technique; I was concerned about the beginning point. Yet the lack of time available and the urgency of the request compelled me to respond.

"God loves you very much and wants you to find God's will even more than you want it," I said.

"Do you really believe that?" she asked.

"I do."

"Well, if I want to find God's will and God wants me to find it, how do we get together? And why is it so difficult for us to recognize?"

As we finished the meal I suggested that God is gentle, like a good parent, and that the coming of the divine presence has a subtlety and ease about it that protects our freedom. Furthermore, I suggested that we embrace God's will with a certain amount of risk; it comes without blueprints or diagrams. I explained that sometimes we have more assurance in retrospect than in prospect.

I felt awkward with this much conversation, suggesting so many ideas in such a brief period. As we parted I hinted that her very consciousness of a desire for God's will could become a beginning point for her to listen, to explore, and to respond.

Behind each of the remarks I made to Joane lies a deep conviction about God's relation to us human beings, a conviction informed by the Judeo-Christian faith. This content of faith provides the convictional base for all our images of the will of God and why we even seek to discover it. The narrative about the origin and destiny of the human race provides the context for our discernment of the divine will.

The Will of God—Source of Being

Behind the affirmations I shared with Joane is the conviction that we exist by and in the will of God, a conviction that finds its support in the opening pages of Genesis.

"In the beginning God created the heavens and the earth" (Gen. 1:1). All statements about the beginning of things are speculative and must be products of a creative imagination. The biblical record assumes that once upon a time there was only God. This conjecture leads to the edge of mystery where God meets us, revealing the divine presence and mysterious being of God's self. This divine abyss is filled with mystery, wonder, and awe.

Out of this eternal depth God spoke: "Let there be light" (1:3). It is the will of God to create. God speaks. God expresses God's will, and all things are created.

"And God saw that it was good" (1:12). All that God

created was good. What God wills is good because God wills it.

"Then God said, 'Let us make man in our image, after our likeness' " (1:26). God willed for us human beings to share the divine nature, to be like God.

The psalmist exclaimed of this creation of God:

Yet thou hast made him little less than God,
    and dost crown him with glory and honor.
Thou hast given him dominion over the works of thy hands;
    thou hast put all things under his feet,
all sheep and oxen,
    and also the beasts of the field,
the birds of the air, and the fish of the sea,
    whatever passes along the paths of the sea.

O LORD, our Lord,
    how majestic is thy name in all the earth!
                              (Psalm 8:5–9)

"And they heard the sound of the LORD God walking in the garden in the cool of the day" (Gen. 3:8). Does not this capacity to hear the sound of God suggest that Adam had an immediate awareness of the divine, that the communion was open and face to face? God willed for this temporal creature, made in the divine image, to have fellowship with God's self. In this pristine state no dissonance existed between Creator and creature. The creature existed in and by the will of God.

The story continues. "But the serpent said" (3:4). Through deception and aroused desire the creature began to question the divine intention, the will of God became suspect, and human beings chose their own will instead of the will of God.

With this decision the comedy of Creation became the tragedy of the Fall. The creatures who saw the Lord God walking in the garden no longer had a clear vision. Rather, both the man and the woman saw only forms in a fog. The intimacy of the original relation gave way to distance and absence. God seemed hidden behind a cloud; the language of God was forgotten. The intention written in the soul became difficult to read. The state of the man and the woman could best be described as one of confusion, darkness, uncertainty, and quest.

"But the LORD God called to the man" (3:9). Sin and disobedience may have violated the will of God, but they could not destroy it. The consequences were tragic: alienation from God, self, and each other. This breakdown in inward and outward harmony also shattered the immediate perception of the will of God and the wholeness that Adam and Eve knew by living in the will of God. Still, the Lord God called to Adam and Eve, never willing for their radical failure to disrupt the eternal purpose.

If we take this narrative of origins as a paradigm, how does it illuminate Joane Welke's experience and yours and mine in our quest for the will of God in our lives? Does this story explain the strong drive for the will of God and the importance of discernment in our individual and corporate lives? Each of us exists because of the will of God; God creates and sustains us each moment of our lives. Being is good; "and God saw that it was good." Whatever Joane's experience with alcoholic parents, a broken marriage, and a failed vocation may have felt like on occasion, discernment operates from the conviction of God's goodness and the goodness of life itself.

Joane's experience of failure and brokenness finds grounding in the trauma of the Fall. She, like Adam and Eve, knew the sense of distance between herself and God. Her question about God's will for her life arose because she could not look within herself and see the divine plan; she did not know a face-to-face relation with God that was free of distortion. All of us know this alienation from self and God; we all experience the uncertainty of what our lives are to be and what choices we should make. This confusion regarding the will of God for our lives creates the need for discernment.

Joane had asked specifically about God's will for her. Why had she been concerned? Why did the question matter to her? The Genesis story states that the Creator called to the creature. Her voicing of the question is but the echo of the divine call that had come to her in her alienation.

What difference does it make how we read the first three

chapters of Genesis? Whether we take them as history, ancient story, or psychological description of the birth of consciousness, the revelation of God seems unaltered. The will of God called the cosmos into being; God's will sustains all creation; the violation of God's will does not destroy it or render God impotent; though violated, the divine will persists in new forms, in difficult, even adverse, circumstances; the will of God, always unconscious in nature, presents itself to human beings, first unconsciously and then consciously in a variety of forms, dialects, accents, and visions.

The divine will is God present with us in the moment; it is Emmanuel here and now. It comes to us wearing many faces, speaking the message of God through many voices. In its myriad presentations we are met again and again; as we learn one dialect the voice changes, introducing us to yet another language of God.

This will of God is good. Being God in our midst, it can be no less; it is the divine presence waiting to be incarnate in our particular choices and actions. To discern the divine presence, to listen to the call, leads to the highest good, the noblest action, and to our ultimate fulfillment. No less does it mean the fulfillment of almighty God. God is fulfilled when God's will is done on earth as it is in heaven. Fulfilling God's will provides the Creator an everlasting memory preserved through the ages.

The Drama of the Divine Intention

Perhaps the search for the will of God can be made more visual through the use of an allegory. Once upon a time there was a citizen of a certain community who concerned himself with the will of God. Let us call him Will B. Dunn, to borrow the name of the comic-strip character from *Kudzu,* created by Doug Marlette. It was rumored in the city that one could find the will of God at the Quad-Life Theater. Will went.

On entering the lobby he looked to his left, and there in the corner he noted the entrance to the Theater of the Absurd. On stage were plays by Jean-Paul Sartre and Samuel Beckett.

On alternate evenings the audience also listened to readings from Martin Heidegger and Karl Jaspers. The theme that was reinforced each evening was "There is no will to be done."

Adjacent to the first theater Will saw the Theater of Science and Technology. On its stage witnesses lauded the unending progress of science and technology; human ingenuity and creativity received applause. The drama, beginning with Aristotle and the Greeks, traced the quest of the human spirit through the Enlightenment and described the discoveries of Copernicus, Newton, Darwin, and Einstein. The theme of this drama was "Our will be done." Will looked further.

Slightly to his right Will noted the American Success Theater. This stage play enacted the founding of the nation, the Revolutionary War for freedom, and the road to wealth, success, and fame. The marquee over the entrance included such names as Ford, Rockefeller, Duke, and Du Pont. The billboards on the wall displayed pictures of Iacocca, Trump, and a dozen other modern-day tycoons. The play promised to show members of the audience how they could make a success of their lives. The play's motto was "My will be done."

Will B. Dunn had no interest in the Theater of the Absurd, nor did the technology of the modern world entice him. He had tasted the drama of success and had decided that this was not the route to meaning for him. Only one theater remained, the Theater of Faith. These characters were dubbed "the kingdom players." Something about the ad attracted his attention and stirred faint hopes. He entered the theater, took a seat, and prepared to review the drama of faith. Above the stage hung a sign that read "Thy will be done."

As Will prepared to watch the play, he took from his pocket a small notebook and pencil; he summarized each act as follows, so he could review it later.

Act I: The Divine Passion

Witnesses to the faith claim that God—the "Divine Mystery, the Creative Depths of Being, the Holy One"—wills to become incarnate in human flesh. This wholly Other intends to take up residence in human consciousness, in human community, in human choices and actions.

In sovereign freedom, God said, "Let there be . . . ," and that initiative called the cosmos into being. This world, called into being by and for God, has become the theater for the production of the drama of the divine intention. The world is not God, yet God sustains and inhabits it. The voice that spoke the world into being continues to whisper through every atom, every mass of energy, every nerve and cell and fiber of creation; everything that exists has the capacity to echo the divine word, to reflect a glimpse of the holy, and to make manifest the will of God.

In this world, this place of things and people, the intention of God happens. On this stage God intends the miracle to occur. Perhaps there could have been a better stage, on which there are no tidal waves or earthquakes or little children born deformed, but one fact remains clear and indisputable: whatever worlds there may have been, this is the world that is. In this world we must discern and fulfill God's will for our time and place, so that the divine mystery becomes flesh in our time.

Act II: Tragedy and Beyond

In the world that houses the divine intention, human beings are the chief actors. When the face-to-face intimacy was broken, the Creator turned reconciler and reestablished the relationship.

God first called out to the original pair, "Where are you?" Later, God called Abram. "Go from your country and your kindred and your father's house to the land that I will show you. And I will make of you a great nation, and I will bless you, and make your name great, so that you will be a blessing. I will bless those who bless you, and him who curses you I will curse; and by you all the families of the earth shall bless themselves" (Gen. 12:1–3). God chose a person and, through him, a nation that would accomplish the divine will. This community, Israel, was intended to be an incarnation of God's will, a light to the world, a voice to the nations.

With this chosen people, God established a covenant; God promised to be their God. To them God gave the law and the commandments. Failure, sin, judgment, and restoration marked their history. Their story revealed most clearly the faithfulness of God and an irrepressible, divine persistence to fulfill the divine will in a community of persons. Their history indicated the patience and persistence of God to become incarnate in a historical community.

The chosen nation, marred with disobedience and unfaithfulness, bore the divine intention in a faithful remnant. The intention of God finally came to clear focus in one faithful man, Christ Jesus. In this one faithful seed of Abram, God fulfilled the promise made generations before by becoming flesh (John 1:14). The divine intention, which came as energy in creation, took personal form in Jesus of Nazareth. In this person the will of God manifested itself in visible, tangible, discernible form. Jesus, the Christ, is the will of God made visible in our history. To encounter him is to encounter God's will. To obey him is to perform God's will. To express his spirit is to incarnate the will of God in history.

Act III: The New Day

Christ, crucified and risen, comes into the consciousness of his faithful followers in the power of the Holy Spirit. This Spirit, the living presence of Christ, shaped the disciples of Jesus into a community and continued in them as divine energy and illumination. Jesus promised that this Spirit would guide the community, teach it, and empower it to do God's will. In the disciple band the passionate intention of God to become flesh was realized in community. In its words and witness, sacraments and rituals, fellowship and worship it intended to express the divine presence. For in all these actions it mediates the divine intention in the world.

But the intention of God, which first expressed itself in creation and again in the restoration, does not end in the church. It aims to conform society and the nations to the will of God revealed in Christ. Discipleship, which develops in the community of faith, strengthens and enriches the church but aims for a new age, a new world in the will of God.

Christ and Will B. Dunn

The play ended. The last character's words still rang in Will's ear: "Life is a stage and you are an actor."

Before Will realized what was happening, the director spoke from behind the curtain. "Will, Will B. Dunn, come up here."

Too startled to move, Will sat frozen in his seat. Again, the call came.

Will struggled to get up. Finally, he made his way to the stage. A voice whispered in his ear, "This is your life; this is the stage upon which you will play it out; the time is now; the place is here."

An Honest Question

After this excursion to the Quad-Life Theater the reader may ask, "What has all this background to do with my simple question, What is the will of God for me?"

The question of the will of God for each of us must be dealt with against the background of the character of the God who wills and the content of that will. This perspective saves the serious inquirer from absorption in his or her own security and personal fulfillment. Yet this larger vision does not cancel God's will for individuals. The will of God for the individual finds its home in the will of God for the whole of creation. An exclusive emphasis on either of these complementary poles distorts God's intention.

A vision of God's action in the whole of human history, such as Will B. Dunn had in the Theater of Faith, calls forth an alternative world. The question of the will of God makes sense only in a world inhabited by the living God. In this kind of world, human freedom matters and personal and social changes are possible through a transformative encounter between the human and the divine. The real world is material, but it is more; it is more than naturalistic evolution; it is more than a playground for scientists and industrialists. The world is a theater in which the drama of the divine will is being enacted or violated in the lives of all living souls.

The Christian perspective on the world offers a vision of the meaning of life and the goals for those who seek God's will. Without this perspective we would be left adrift on a sea of vague feelings and hungers.

When, therefore, we ask, "What is the will of God for me?" this question must be understood within the context of what God has revealed through Israel, Christ, and the church. Our answer must be part of the fleshing out of the divine intention on this stage at this time.

How do human beings discern the divine intention for their lives? The Theater of Faith claimed that Christ was the incarnation of the will of God; in him the will of God became visible.

Whether the questioner is Joane Welke, Will B. Dunn, you, or me, we are all confronted with the question of how we discern the will of God in a way that preserves our freedom and integrity. Does it come in loud voices? Is it coded in rules and regulations? These are the kinds of questions our estrangement from God creates, and these are the questions we must answer in our quest for meaning, a disguised quest for the will of God.

Even when we know God's will as revealed in Christ, we still must give it specific shape. We know, for example, that we are to love our neighbor, but what form does love take? The creative imagination shapes the divine will into specific behaviors. *What* we are to do and *how* we are to do it require discernment.

The creative imagination depends not only on data from the present but also on memory. Discernment depends on the accumulated learnings of life. Perhaps the combined power of intuition and imagination enables us to discern the divine action expressed in our lives. Discernment for our future depends on the careful attention to the ways of God in our past.

In each of us there is a compelling "ought." Some behaviors are moral imperatives. In some instances we may have no previous experience, no positive models. Nevertheless, we have a conviction about the direction we should take. Despite the cultural pollution of this sense of "ought," it can be informed and refined until it provides directives that are expressive of the divine intention. Yet no matter how profoundly we are grasped with an ought, the concrete act of obedience always contains a risk—the risk of specific choice, the risk of our interpretation, the risk of an unpredictable outcome. In some profound way we come to know by doing.

Can we believe that each person has a part to play in the great cosmic drama? Can God's will be done on earth? Can the great eternal purpose of God be fulfilled? Will we seek to glorify God, do God's will on earth as it is done in heaven?

If these questions arouse us, we ask, "How can I discern God's will for my life, for all of my life?"

The meaning of our lives, a quest in which we all engage, must be discovered in a larger context than our personal consciousness; it must be found in the context of God's cosmic purpose for creation and human history. Just as the answer to Joane Wilke's life is to be found in the larger arena of God's intention for creation, surely our own meanings must derive from this larger understanding of the world. In Will B. Dunn we met ourselves in the choices of our own lives and the ready options.

Will B. Dunn's experience in the Theater of Faith creates the context and opens up the issues that confront all of us in the quest for the meaning of our lives. Beginning with the historical Christ, it is my intention to explore with you the norm of discernment and to see how the faculties of the soul function to discern God's will for our lives.

Three

The Will of God Made Flesh

Imagine that you have survived a shipwreck. Broken apart in the storm, the ship went down, and you were the lone person with a life jacket and a raft. After days of treacherous battle with the sea, you were finally washed up on an inhabited island.

After days of drying out and recovering from your ordeal you realize that you have been rescued by a group of people with a culture very different from your own. You begin to learn their language. Soon they indicate to you that in order to be one of them, you must learn to do their special dance.

One of the more aggressive of the clan tells you to dance. "Dance the lapa-lapa," he says.

But I don't know how to do the lapa-lapa, you think to yourself. I've never seen the lapa-lapa; I don't know anyone who does the lapa-lapa.

Your new friends urge you to dance the lapa-lapa and tell you that you cannot become part of their culture unless you do. Finally, you try. You first move your feet and then your arms; you add the swaying of your body like a palm tree bowing to the wind.

The clan laughs at you. "That's not the lapa-lapa."

At last the oldest member comes to your rescue. She eases

over to you and speaks to you in your embarrassment. "I will tell you how to do the lapa-lapa," she says.

She describes the movements to make. When you look dumbfounded she moves with the rhythm of the wind, showing you all the key movements of the dance.

You begin to move with her. She suggests a few corrections to your bumbling efforts. When you don't correct your steps she comes to you, places her arms around you, and dances with you. Never discouraged, she keeps dancing with you until you master the intricate movements.

Is not learning to do the will of God something like this? You awaken from the darkness of unconsciousness. Something inside cries out for meaning, but you do not know your life's meaning or how to find it. With all your strenuous efforts you cannot discover the meaning of your life; you know neither its structure nor its content. Without understanding the meaning of your life, how can you fulfill it?

Into this frustration and turmoil comes Christ. He is the will of God made flesh. To use the metaphor of the dance, he enables us to dance the dance of God. He demonstrates the dance to us. When we do not understand, he instructs us again and again. If our efforts still fail, he takes us in his arms and dances with us until we can do the dance of God.

The metaphor of the dance opens for us the questions that must be asked about the will of God:

What is the will of God?
How can I recognize it?
What norm can be used to judge what is, or is not, the will of God?

Or, to use the metaphor of the dance, "How can I learn to do the dance of God?"

As Christians we begin with the confession that the will of God was made concrete in the person of Jesus. His own statements suggest that he lived in an awareness of this unique vocation. The Fourth Gospel, in contrast to the other three, gives special attention to his self-consciousness: that is, who Jesus perceived himself to be. In this gospel Jesus makes a number of daring claims that fuse his earthly life with the will of God. For example, Jesus said to his followers, "I am not of this world." His origin was not from nature, and this self-affirmation agrees with the prologue: "In the beginning was the Word, and the Word was with God, and the Word was God" (John 1:1).

To the Jews, Jesus said, "I have come down from heaven, not to do my own will, but the will of him who sent me" (6:38). He exposed his purpose for coming as doing the will of God, and his actions manifested that will. If he did the will of God in his life, the record of his deeds and teachings offers an objective norm, a concrete description of the divine intention.

Jesus made his identification with God even more explicit. "I and the Father are one" (10:30). Toward the end of his ministry Jesus explained this declaration with two rhetorical questions: "Have I been with you so long, and yet you do not know me?" And, "Do you not believe that I am in the Father and the Father in me? The words that I say to you I do not speak on my own authority; but the Father who dwells in me does his works" (14:9–10). What could Jesus have said to make his identification with God more explicit? If we believe the writer of the Fourth Gospel, the person of Jesus—and thus his words and actions—provides a visible demonstration of the intention of the invisible God.

This claim of Jesus leaves us only with a question of his integrity. Can Jesus' statements about himself be trusted? In one of his encounters with the Jews, Jesus also dealt with this issue. When they questioned whether he knew God, Jesus responded, "If I said I do not know him, I should be a liar" (John 8:55). Jesus cannot deny his intimate knowledge of God and be true to his own being; to speak otherwise would violate his personhood.

These statements of Jesus convince me that he is identified with the will of God; he is the visible expression of the invisible will of God. He provided a human medium through which we encounter the divine will. We encounter in Jesus of Nazareth the will of God made flesh. Claiming this of Jesus does not exhaust the revelation, nor does it offer the only approach to the incarnation. But if we understand him as the will of God made flesh, we have a clear norm for the discernment of God's will—the life and teachings of Jesus of Nazareth.

From this perspective we will explore the metaphors that Jesus applied to himself as expressive of the divine will in our lives, we will analyze the content of God's will in Jesus' teaching and ministry, we will examine the style in which God's will comes to us through the actions of Christ, and, finally, we will examine the manner in which the Spirit internalizes the will of God in us.

In the metaphor of the dance, these explorations into the life of Jesus enable us to visualize the dance and to know the content of the dance, the various styles of the dance, and even the rhythm of the dance. Certainly, of the infinite number of possibilities for the dance, doing the dance of God requires discernment.

The Metaphors of God's Will

If Jesus is the will of God made flesh, the metaphors that he applied to himself provide us with insight into the nature of the divine will. The metaphors enable us to look more deeply into the way that Jesus Christ provides a norm for discerning the will of God in our lives.

A metaphor, like a window, permits us to penetrate a barrier to our vision. The windows in a sea aquarium permit visitors to peer into the giant tank at different levels. No single window offers a complete view of everything in the tank, but each provides a slightly different perspective with additional content. The metaphors Jesus used to describe himself are like that. Each provides a slightly different perspective and opens up the will of God more fully. Perhaps the metaphors of bread, light, shepherd, door, servant, vine, and way can indeed clarify dimensions of the will of God in our lives.

The first metaphor of himself that Jesus used was bread. After feeding the five thousand he explained to the multitude and the disciples, "I am the bread of life" (John 6:35). If Jesus is the will of God made flesh, his designation of himself as bread points toward sustenance. The will of God nourishes the soul, provides energy, and generates strength; it satisfies the human hunger for nourishment and gives delight. The will of God, under the metaphor of bread, fills our deepest needs and satisfies our deepest longings.

When a missionary friend every day exposes himself to the crying needs of poor people, and when he sees an oppressive government that is unresponsive to their pain, what keeps him going? Does he not draw energy from the call of God, the fact that God has placed him in this country to be an expression of Christ? Is not the bread of God's will the nourishment that sustains him?

Jesus referred to himself as the light of the world (John 8:12). Light illuminates; without it even healthy eyes cannot see. Light exposes the path or the road for persons to travel from one place to another. When the will of God, like light, illuminates the mind, persons are able to see the direction of their lives.

The will of God, under the metaphor of light, shows us the path, the course, the way. In the deeper sense, Christ, as the will of God, enables us to understand the will of God and discern the course to choose.

We are familiar with the darkness in which Augustine lived for years. Under the preaching of Ambrose he was awakened from his sleep. Then one day, in a mysterious way, he heard the voice of a little child saying, "Take, read; take, read." He picked up the Bible and read:

> Let us then cast off the works of darkness and put on the armor of light; let us conduct ourselves becomingly as in the day, not in reveling and drunkenness, not in debauchery and licentiousness, not in quarreling and jealousy. But put on the Lord Jesus Christ, and make no provision for the flesh, to gratify its desires.
>
> (Romans 13:12–14)

That day the will of God came to him as light, instructing him as to the course to take. It came with such convincing force that his life was changed.

Jesus states that he is the door to the sheepfold. A door provides an entrance, a passage from the outside to the inside, from one room to another. A doorway not only provides an opening but also offers closure. When it opens the way into the future, it also provides closure on the past.

The will of God, as a doorway, provides an alternative; it offers an entrance into a new life and, at the same time, closes off the old. When a person suffers loss or cold or confusion, a door brings relief and hope. Jesus, in his person, offers this new opportunity. This ministry of Jesus reminds us of Paul's affirmation, "But I will stay in Ephesus until Pentecost, for a wide door for effective work has opened to me, and there are many adversaries" (1 Cor. 16:8–9). Paul describes the will of God for his work as a door being opened to him.

Paul speaks again of the door as an opening to do the will of God: "When I came to Troas to preach the gospel of Christ, a door was opened for me in the Lord" (2 Cor. 2:12). Paul often associated the door with an opportunity to preach the gospel, but for him the door clearly expressed the will of God.

The apostle John, on the isle of Patmos, heard the risen Christ speak to the church at Philadelphia: "I have set before you an open door, which no one is able to shut" (Rev. 3:8). Again, this metaphor of the door points to opportunity to do the will of God.

In another metaphor, Jesus described himself as "the good shepherd" (John 10:11). He elaborated the role of the shepherd: the shepherd knows his sheep; he calls them by name; he goes before them; he leads them out and helps them find nourishment. If one gets lost, he searches for it until he finds it (Luke 15:4–6).

Can we image the will of God as a shepherd to the soul? This metaphor suggests the warm, intimate, personal dimension of the will of God. The will of God, like the shepherd, comes to us; it knows who we are; it speaks our name; it lays out the path before us and attends us on the journey. If we stray from it, it seeks us out. Like a good shepherd, the will of God takes hold of us and will not let us go. Jesus, the good shepherd, embodies the will of God for us in this manner.

Perhaps the will of God as shepherd of the soul can be most appreciated when we have failed to do God's will. Was not Jesus that kind of shepherd for Peter when Peter met him on the beach after the crucifixion?

Peter had denied the Lord. He and his companions had gone back to their old vocation of fishing. All night they had fished and caught nothing. About dawn they saw a figure on the beach. It was Jesus.

Peter plunged into the water. When Peter met Jesus, not a word of condemnation came from him. In the face of Peter's failure, Jesus asked, "Peter, do you love me?" Is that not shepherdlike?

Jesus used another metaphor of himself that also illuminates the will of God, the metaphor of servant Jesus said, "I am among you as one who serves" (Luke 22:27). The notion of the will of God coming to us as a servant, at first glance, contradicts our understanding of the nature of God. Have we not thought of God as one who comes against us, makes demands on us, even calls us to serve? Without denying this aspect of God's nature, can we believe that God also serves us, serves our highest good? To serve means to submit oneself to another, to care for his or her best interests. Can this describe the will of God?

As contradictory as it may sound, Jesus, who came to do God's will, demonstrated God as a servant of humanity. How else can we explain the scene in the upper room when Jesus takes the basin and towel and stoops before the disciples? One by one he washes their feet. He claims to be among them as one who serves. Does not the will of God serve us by satisfying our deepest needs? The divine will, by serving us, inspires the spirit of servanthood and thereby empowers us to serve as we have been served by God.

Yet another metaphor that Jesus applied to himself illuminates the will of God. Jesus used the metaphor of the vine and the branches to describe his relation with his followers. The vine provides nourishment for the branches; it is their strength. For this reason, Jesus said, "Apart from me you can do nothing" (John 15:5). The branches must remain connected to the vine to have life and productivity. If a branch does not remain connected to the vine, it is cast forth and withers.

Does not this metaphor underscore human dependency on the will of God? When we abide in God's will, we have the power to do what that will dictates. Estranged from that will, life withers and dies. Jesus encouraged an unconditional confidence in prayer to those who remain in God's will: "If you abide in me, and my words abide in you, ask whatever you will, and it shall be done for you" (John 15:7).

In our own experience, the image of the plug and the electrical outlet illustrates dependence on God. As long as the cord is plugged into the source, energy flows through the wire, but when the cord is unplugged, the energy disappears. This metaphor seems to be directed to all servants of God. If we remain united to Christ, to the will of God, the energy flows through our efforts. But when we turn our service toward ourselves or seek to perform it by our own power, the energy of God disappears. Could this explain why so many of God's servants experience burnout?

In another powerful metaphor, Jesus spoke of himself as resurrection. Jesus said, "I am the resurrection and the life" (John 11:25). If we perceive the will of God as resurrection, it is able to bring life out of death. Are we not dead to God without the activation of God's will in us?

Possibly Paul had this metaphor in mind when he wrote to the Ephesians, "And you he made alive, when you were dead through the trespasses and sins in which you once walked, following the course of this world, following the prince of the power of the air, the spirit that is now at work in the sons of disobedience" (Eph. 2:1–2). Christ as the will of God was the power of resurrection for these persons.

In the last of the metaphors, Jesus gathered the insights of the other six: "I am the way, and the truth, and the life" (John 14:6). The way speaks of a direction and style, the truth aims at what is real and lasting, and the life speaks of final meaning and fulfillment. Jesus, as the way, the truth, and the life, raises us to life out of death; offers us nourishment that feeds our hunger like bread; illuminates our minds with truth; exposes the pathway before us as light; opens an entrance into new pathways and closes old ones as the door; strengthens, guides, and protects our lives like a shepherd; serves us as a hired hand; and makes our lives productive like a vine.

These metaphors enable us to grasp different aspects of God's will. What do they say to us about discernment? Can we not look at our life experience through these lenses to judge the will of God by its life-giving power, nourishment, and illumination, opening new possibilities, extending care and service, sustaining and bearing fruit? Although metaphors never speak with precision (that would contradict the nature of the metaphor), they do create a context in which more precise judgments about the specific content of God's will may be made. If metaphors provide a context, or if they serve like windows to reveal glimpses of the will of God, we still need more specific guidance concerning the content of the will of God. What did Jesus say was God's will? What did Jesus do to demonstrate the will of God?

The Content of God's Will

If we take Jesus as the will of God made flesh, guidance for decisions comes not only from the metaphors that he applied to himself but also from the content of his actions and teachings. An examination of the teachings and actions of Jesus, as set forth in this Fourth Gospel, suggests that God wills persons to be whole, that they love and serve one another, continue the work of Christ, and live in unity.

The Gospel of John makes clear that God wills persons to be whole—spiritually, physically, and emotionally. Jesus summed up this aspect of God's will in a single statement: "I came that [you] may have life, and have it abundantly" (John 10:10). True life—life freed from its insensitivity to God, life expunged from its guilt and self-condemnation, life healed of inferiority and disease—this is God's will revealed in Christ.

Not only did Jesus declare in words that God willed wholeness, but he made persons whole. A religious leader, Nicodemus, came to him inquiring as to who he was. Jesus seemingly disregarded his questions and spoke to the burning issue of Nicodemus' life. The conversation produced new life, a "new birth" in Nicodemus. Indeed, God wills persons to be awakened to the divine presence. This birth of the Spirit makes persons aware of the presence and of the importance of God's will for their lives.

Jesus encountered a paralytic on Solomon's porch (John 5). He asked if the man wanted to be made whole. So accustomed was the paralytic to rationalizing the situation that he began to explain why he was still ill, having been in that condition for thirty-eight years. Then Jesus reached out and touched the man, telling him to arise and go home.

The centurion's son, being healed, further makes us aware that God wills illness to be overcome (John 4:46–54). Each of these encounters with Jesus makes it clear that God wills for persons to have life in its fullness. In our own lives and in the lives of others, we should always identify the will of God with health, wholeness, and completeness.

God also wills that we love one another. Nothing has been made clearer in the life and teaching of Jesus than the ethic of love. In his closing remarks to his followers, Jesus said, "This is my commandment, that you love one another as I have loved you" (15:12). Again, "This I command you, to love one another" (15:17). In word and example, Jesus disclosed that God's will always demanded love. In Jesus, love was expressed as forgiveness (Mark 2:5), as an attitude of "no condemnation" (John 8:1–11), as "serving others" (5:5–13), and finally in the sacrifice of himself for those whom he loved (19:28–30).

In addition to love in all our relationships, God intends us to serve one another. This image of the divine will became explicit when Jesus took the towel and basin and washed the disciples' feet (John 13:1–11). When he finished he said to them, "If I then, your Lord and Teacher, have washed your feet, you also ought to wash one another's feet" (13:14). In this specific command, Jesus summed up the theme of servanthood that had characterized his life.

The content of God's will also includes doing the works of Christ—whatever we see Christ doing, we are to do. He told his followers that "he who believes in me will also do the works that I do" (John 14:12). Jesus' works provide the criteria by which we discern the will of God, because it is God's will that we do the same works of love in our day that Jesus did when he was here in the flesh.

Along with wholeness, love, service, and doing the kind of deeds that Jesus did, God also wills that the followers of Christ become one—the unity of all Christians. Christ prayed "that they may all be one; even as thou, Father, art in me, and I in thee, that they also may be in us, so that the world may believe that thou hast sent me" (John 17:21). In our relations with all believers, love expresses itself in unity. Every division in the fellowship of believers violates God's intention.

This specific content provides guidance in discerning the will of God. In cases of illness and suffering, God always wills wholeness. Where spiritual deadness and unawareness exist, God wills spiritual life. In all our relations, God wills love. Where human need exists, God wills our service. What we perceive in Christ, God wills us also to do; and God wills the unity of all believers. These definitive expressions of God's will provide criteria for us to discern the shape of God's will for our lives.

The revelation of the will of God in Christ holds universal significance, but the specifics of how this will is to be enacted are left open. For example, Christ tells us to "love one another," but he leaves open to our discretion and freedom the manner of love. He tells us to serve but does not fill out the specifics of our service. So we know the parameters of God's will, but the details of shape and mode are left up to human discernment and freedom.

The Style of God's Will

Identifying Jesus as the will of God incarnate has enabled us to illuminate the divine will through the metaphors that Christ applied to himself; this identification has also provided us specific content of God's will through Jesus' example and instruction. Jesus as the will of God incarnate offers yet another insight—the manner in which the will of God comes to us. We might call this the style, or the etiquette, of the divine will that we discover in Jesus' approach to people.

Even though we know the content of God's will is wholeness or love or service, the call to specific responses in specific circumstances can be confusing, especially when two demands come into conflict. For example, a man has been commanded to love his wife, as an expression of God's will; he has also been commanded to serve the poor. He finds himself torn between loving his wife, and responding to her needs, and visiting widows who are sick and shut in. How is he to discern the will of God in the tension created by conflicting obligations? Some light will be thrown on this and similar questions by the model of Jesus' interaction because these encounters provide models of how the will of God engages us.

The will of God challenges us to investigate the facts. When the will of God presents itself to us in the form of a call or directive, God is not offended by hesitancy and uncertainty. In that vague situation the Lord invites us to explore the meaning and the risk of the call and to anticipate the possible outcome.

This divine etiquette shows itself in Jesus' invitation to the disciples of John the Baptist. The Baptist had identified Jesus to his disciples. A few of them followed Jesus and spoke to him.

"Rabbi, where are you staying?"

Jesus responded, "Come and see" (see John 1:39).

The will of God always stands up under investigation. The will of God does not demand a blind, ignorant response but affords space for questioning and groping.

This same principle can also be seen in Ananias' wrestling with the commission to go to Saul (Acts 9:11–15). Probably Ananias had the vision in his time of prayer. The Lord called his name. Ananias responded, "Here I am, Lord."

When he was instructed to go to the street called Straight and inquire about Saul, he reacted negatively. He reasoned with the Lord that Saul had come to imprison and kill believers in Damascus.

But the Lord spoke again: "Go, for he is a chosen instrument of mine to carry my name before the Gentiles and kings and the sons of Israel" (Acts 9:15). Ananias went.

Note, however, that the Lord made space for Ananias' fears. He permitted him to reason, even to resist. Such is the nature of the divine will. It comes to us with enough strength to handle our resistance; it will hold up under our questioning. Even when rejected it has the resilience to bounce back repeatedly into our consciousness.

The will of God often manifests an alluring, seductive side. The divine will captures our imagination and entices our desires, causing us to pursue it. Yet the divine attraction never abuses human freedom. When the divine will comes into our consciousness it speaks, but the voice does not muffle our own. We inquire, and the Spirit says, "Look. Examine. Discriminate." The divine will makes room for human freedom and involvement in discernment and performance.

The will of God also comes to us as affirmation. The writer of the Fourth Gospel states it clearly: "God sent the Son into the world, not to condemn the world, but that the world might be saved through him" (John 3:17).

This principle finds no clearer explication than in Jesus' encounter with the woman accused of adultery (John 8:1–11). He asks, "Woman, where are they [your accusers]? Has no one condemned you?" She said, "No one, Lord."

Jesus responded, "Neither do I condemn you."

Many of us have been trained in a religious environment that made the will of God negative. A long list of "thou shalt nots" provided the dominant image of God's will. Yet in looking at the will of God made flesh, we discover that Jesus' way was affirmation. He built on what was good; he directed his disciples positively; even his rebuke was gentle. Dare we believe that God's will comes to us in this positive, wholesome manner?

Possibly in no other place do we need conversion so much as in our expectations concerning God's will. Perhaps we should begin to suspect the evil one as a "nagger," the instigator of bad conscience and the purveyor of unreal guilt. And we should begin to pay attention to the subtle intuitions to love, to serve, and to forgive.

Stated positively, the will of God meets us in love. As he left the disciples, Jesus said to them, "I do not say to you that I shall pray the Father for you; for the Father himself loves you, because you have loved me and have believed that I came from the Father" (John 16:26–27). If God, as Father, loves us as deeply as the revelation in Jesus suggests, the divine will can only come to us in love.

When the will of God has the character of love, it comes with patience and kindness; it is never rude (1 Cor. 13:4–5). The divine will never ends; in comparison with all other virtues, it is the greatest (13:8, 13).

Consider also that the will of God comes to us when we have been prepared. When Jesus was in Jerusalem after Passover, many believed in him when they saw the signs he did; but Jesus did not trust himself to them (John 2:24). Jesus knew human nature and perceived that some were unprepared for the will of God. Were he to reveal God's will to them, they would either ignore it, pervert it, distort it, or betray it; therefore, it was withheld from them. Human readiness for the divine will does not alter God's intention but does condition the time of disclosure.

The issue of preparation seems to be woven into the fabric of revelation: Israel was prepared, the mother of Jesus was prepared, and the early church was prepared to receive the divine will through the Spirit. Preparation meant making the recipient ready to perceive God's special working. The will of God meets us in the concrete issues of our lives, in the matters that concern us. Most often our personal history has prepared us to receive the divine will.

Perhaps the style of the will of God can be summed up in the encounter of Jesus with the Samaritan woman (John 4:1–30). The style of Jesus in this encounter provides a paradigm of the manner in which the will of God comes to us. A clear understanding of the style will empower us in discerning God's action. Notice the characteristics of Jesus' encounter with the woman at the well.

Jesus met the woman in the context of her life—in Samaria, at the well. He placed himself in the woman's pathway.

"And so Jesus, wearied as he was with his journey, sat down beside the well" (4:6).

Not only did Jesus place himself where she regularly came, he also took the initiative to engage her. He spoke first. "Give me a drink" (4:7). Then, having gained her attention, he awakened her curiosity. "If you knew . . . who it is that is saying to you, 'Give me a drink,' you would have asked him, and he would have given you living water" (4:10). She was made to wonder. This suggestion opened to her the realm of "what if." This suggestion of Jesus illustrates the lure of the divine will.

Jesus promised the woman fulfillment. "Every one who drinks of this water will thirst again, but whoever drinks of the water that I shall give him will never thirst" (4:13–14). The self-chosen way does not bring lasting fulfillment—only God's way.

Jesus focused on the major issue in the woman's life. "Go, call your husband, and come here" (4:16). She had had five husbands; she was not married to the man with whom she now lived. Behind the moral issue stood this woman's inability to sustain a relationship. Doubtless she experienced failure, low self-esteem, and hopelessness. Jesus sought to bring wholeness to her life.

When she confessed her situation, "I have no husband," Jesus affirmed her. "You are right in saying, 'I have no husband' " (4:17). He affirmed her in telling the truth.

Jesus revealed to her a deeper understanding of God. "God is spirit, and those who worship him must worship in spirit and truth" (4:24). He did not repudiate her knowledge or history but built on it and refined it.

Finally, when she confessed that she expected Messiah, Jesus revealed himself: "I who speak to you am he" (4:26). He assured her of his identity.

Even a dull imagination can transpose this encounter of Jesus with the woman and quickly see the manner in which the will of God engages us. It meets us in our context, it takes the initiative, it promises to fulfill our deepest longings, it meets us most clearly in the major issues of our lives, it affirms us, it opens a deeper understanding of the divine mystery, and in the end it makes clear God's will for us.

This depiction of the style of the divine will obviates those unrealistic ideas that God's will comes to us other than in the context of our lives, creating the illusion that we need to go to another place to find God's will. God's will is *now* and the starting place is *here!*

This model repudiates the notion that we must seek and seek to find God's will. The will of God comes to us; we need only receive it. Jesus shows us the value of discerning receptivity rather than zealous searching.

The style of God denies that the will of God is totally alien to us; it awakens our desires and speaks to our deepest need.

Finally, this revelation of the divine will, or this paradigm, undercuts the skepticism that we can never know the will of God or whether we have done it! The will of God grants an assurance of its true identity—usually, however, in retrospect. To reveal itself too early would repudiate the power and importance of trust.

Thus far we have identified Christ with the will of God; he is God's will made flesh. In this perspective Christ symbolizes God's full intention. This vision of God's will has been opened up by the metaphors Christ applied to himself. To protect these metaphors from abuse, we have recalled specific acts and statements that gave concrete expression to the divine will. And in the final section we have described the style of the will of God as it intersects our lives. This extensive description of the will of God made visible holds enormous importance for those who seek to discern the meaning of their lives. What we see in Christ provides a norm for our discernment; he is the principle, the measuring rod by which we determine God's will.

The Will of God Internalized

At the end of his ministry, Jesus taught his disciples about an extension of this normative principle. Jesus described this extension as counselor, comforter, and Holy Spirit. He promised to send the divine presence after his departure (John 16:7). The Spirit, Jesus explained, would take up residence in his followers (see 14:17). As an indwelling presence, the Spirit would teach the disciples and enable them to recall what Jesus

had taught them (14:26). This relation of the Spirit to Christ
is further linked by Jesus' explanation that the Spirit would
bear witness to him (see 15:26). In addition to witness, the
Spirit guides the disciples into all the truth (16:13), the truth
that had not been stated by Jesus. And this presence within us
must be identified with the living Christ who said, "I will not
leave you desolate; I will come to you" (14:18). Through the
Spirit, the will of God now becomes internalized in the followers of Christ. This internalization of Christ (or the will of God
for us) occurs through the Spirit's ministry within us. This
affirmation returns us to the central question of discernment
and forces us to ask, "How does the Holy Spirit function in the
human psyche to enable us to discern God's will?" Does not
the Spirit act on certain aspects of the psyche, to bring to
consciousness images and intuitions of the divine will?

Because of the suspicion of the Spirit's work in the soul of
a follower of Christ, a suspicion that is beginning to have the
weight of a conviction, we will investigate the various capacities
of the psyche as instruments of discernment under the influence of the Spirit: intuition, imagination, memory, and will.

The role of the Spirit in this act of discernment may be
defined as counselor, guide, or presence of Christ who intends
to reveal the will of God to people in the context of their
existential situations. The validity of this guidance may be mea-
sured in relation to the manifestation of the divine will in the
historical Christ. The ministry of leading us into all truth includes direction in the specific pathways we are to follow and
the goals we are to pursue.

Now we turn to an investigation of the created psyche and
the hidden presence of the will of God in it. We will discover
how these various aspects of the image of God—divine intention, Holy Spirit, the normative Christ—combine and interact
in the concrete circumstances that require discernment.

Four

The Will of God Written in the Soul

The temple was built on an island and it held a thousand bells. Bells big and small, fashioned by the finest craftsman in the world. When the wind blew or a storm raged, all the bells would peal out in a symphony that would send the heart of the hearer into raptures.

But over the centuries the island sank into the sea and with it, the temple bells. An ancient legend said that the bells continued to peal out, ceaselessly, and could be heard by anyone who would listen. Inspired by this legend, a young man traveled thousands of miles, determined to hear those bells. He sat for days on the shore, facing the vanished island, and listened with focused attention. But all he could hear was the sound of the sea. He made every effort to block it out. But to no avail; the sound of the sea seemed to flood the world.

He kept at his task for weeks. Each time he got disheartened he would listen to the village pundits, who spoke with unction of the mysterious legend.

Then his heart would be aflame . . . only to become discouraged again when weeks of further effort yielded no results.

Finally he decided to give up the attempt. Perhaps he was not destined to hear the bells. Perhaps the legend was not

true. It was his final day, and he went to the shore to say
goodbye to the sea and the sky and the wind and the coconut
trees. He lay on the sand, and for the first time, listened to the
sound of the sea. Soon he was so lost in the sound that he was
barely conscious of himself, so deep was the silence that the
sound produced.

In the depth of that silence he heard it! The tinkle of a
tiny bell followed by another, and another and another . . .
and soon every one of the thousand temple bells was pealing
out in harmony, and his heart was rapt in joyous ecstasy.[1]

What have a sunken temple and ringing bells to do with our
discernment of the will of God? Already we have seen that the
driving hunger of human beings is for meaning. We cannot
find this meaning in our own power, though it is our highest
good; this search for meaning is a search for the will of God
that has come to us in a visible form in Jesus of Nazareth.

Pointing to Jesus as the will of God made flesh does not
resolve all our existential questions, nor does it solve our problems of particular choices for our individual lives. The expression of the intention of God in Christ provides a framework
within which to struggle with our questions; it offers us a norm
but not a blueprint. If Jesus is the standard or model for us,
how does God's specific will become flesh in us? We return to
the question at the center of our quest: "How do we discern
God's will?"

Here the story of the temple and the bells brings illumination. According to the legend, the submerged temple contained the bells, the bells continued to ring, but the tones were
heard only by those ears which penetrated the silence to listen.
Perhaps it is also true that, though the temple of God has been
submerged by sin, the bells of that eternal purpose still ring out
but require a deep silence to hear them.

Maybe it is true that the will of God made flesh in Jesus has
been written into the structure of our soul. It is a part of us;
it is our very selves. Thus to fulfill the will of God that is
revealed to us in Jesus simultaneously fulfills our deepest longings inspired by the will of God written in the human heart. To
discern the will of God is to discern our own reason for being.

If we are to trust the remnants of the image of God in the human psyche, it is important to show, from a faith perspective, how the will of God is written into the structure of the soul; to explore the nature of this inner wisdom from a psychological perspective; and to suggest the human capacities for discerning the will of God, noting both the possibilities and the pitfalls of this inner approach to God's will.

The Image of God in the Soul

The Bible speaks of divine intentions and influences that impinge on humanity, influences over which we have no control. For example, we had no control over the powers of creation. None of us was consulted about whether we wanted to be. Through the miracle of the union of sperm and egg, our creation began. The initiation of this miracle of our being lies outside human decision or control. Yet our creation implicitly contains an intention; we were not created for "nothing." Like the bells created by the craftsman to ring, our lives also were created for a purpose.

According to the biblical revelation, we were created in the image of God, in the likeness of the divine (Gen. 1:26–27). An expression of the divine will is certainly intrinsic to the very nature of God. If we are made in the image of God, then we are also bearers of God's will; it is a vital part of the image of God within us.

The divine will not only embraces all humanity in a vague, general way; surely it embraces each individual creature as well. Therefore, in creation each of us has been given potential for being and becoming what God wills. Our very existence has been intertwined with the will of God. Although we have these powers, we must never forget that they are not private possessions; they are continuously given to us by God, as is everything in creation. The creative power of God gives us the potency for participating in the will of God and also intimations of what that will is.

While affirming this creative presence that has marked us with the will of God and empowers us to fulfill it, this image has been marred. In our fall into sin the sensibilities that discern God's will have been blunted, and direct access to this will has been blocked. The powers of creation demonstrate mighty and continuous strength, yet these powers do not restore to human beings a direct approach to the will of God. That temple of God has sunk into the depths of consciousness; it peals out the intention of God, but we have difficulty listening to it or hearing its voice. Even when we hear the tones, they are vague and difficult to decipher.

Deeper reflection on the legend of the bells suggests that the craftsman who created the bells operated with freedom: he obtained the materials for the bells, he designed their shape, and he chose the temple and the place in the temple they would be installed. These choices of the craftsman doubtlessly affected the bells and the tones they would make. The role of the craftsman affected both the tone and the utility of the bells.

Does not the Master Craftsman's decision have some effect on the soul? The apostle Paul said, "Blessed be the God and Father of our Lord Jesus Christ, who has blessed us in Christ with every spiritual blessing in the heavenly places, *even as he chose us in him before the foundation of the world,* that we should be holy and blameless before him" (Eph. 1:3–4, emphasis added).

The Craftsman and Creator of the world has chosen us from the beginning. To be chosen means to be elected by God for God's own purposes. If God desired and chose us, this action cannot be without consequence for God's purpose. Surely the influence of the election of God impinges on the soul, drawing it toward the eternal purpose of God. God's election must indeed be like a magnet that attracts us toward God and the divine intention for our lives. Yet this magnetism operates in a manner that human freedom is neither distorted nor destroyed.

If we humans have been created in the image of God, the shape of creation turns us toward God. Is it not also true that being chosen by God exerts a powerful influence on the soul? Yet this divine choice for us often exerts a power and an influence on us that we cannot name.

Consider again the legend of the vanished temple. The architect of the temple and the craftsman who created the bells had a vision for both. Perhaps they envisioned the temple with its thousand bells pealing out warnings during the storm; or perhaps they visualized the bells as providing pleasant tones in the dusk of the evening, sending the hearer into rapture; or perhaps they saw the temple as a beautiful setting for the worship of God. Whatever their purposes, their efforts were not aimless.

In a similar manner the God who calls us into being and continuously calls us into a relationship has an intention for our lives. God intends us to be conformed to the image of Christ. Again, the great apostle says, "For those whom he foreknew he also predestined to be conformed to the image of his Son, in order that he might be the first-born among many brethren" (Rom. 8:29). The doctrine of predestination, when misunderstood, obviates human freedom and tends toward a static experience of conformity; properly understood, this doctrine speaks of God's intention for all those who have been chosen. If God has destined us for conformity to Christ, certainly this does not mean the emotionless copying of a blueprint without regard for the subject of the copy. Rather, we must recognize that conformity to Christ also means a reunion with that intention for which we were created. Christ has redeemed us not to a life alien to our deepest needs and hungers but to a restored life, the life that God intended. Hints at this original intention are manifest in the inclinations, preferences, and tastes in the subjective experience of each person. Thus to be predestined means to be predisposed, to have certain preferences, and then to be drawn toward strong but undefined goals by the gracious power of God.

If God has made us for a particular purpose, must we not believe that the intended purpose exerts a constant influence on us? Is this intention not written on the soul?

Look again at the legend. The young man in our story came to the edge of despair; he was ready to give up his yearning. Perhaps he was not destined to hear the bells; maybe the story was not true. He came to his final day. By some stroke of fate or luck or providence he decided to go to the beach one last time. This time as he sat on the sand he listened to the sound of the sea. Absorbed in the sounds he sank into a deep silence, and in the silence he heard the tinkle of a tiny bell. What caused him to go to the sea this one last time?

Could we not call this last effort an act of providence? Providence activates and gives specific content to the divine intention in creation that has been drawn forward by election and propelled by predestination. Providence speaks of those workings of the Spirit of God both within the human soul and in the events of personal life that provide specific invitations to actualize the will of God in concrete choices. Apart from actual situations in life that evoke our choices, the will of God remains localized in God's self or in a vague, subjective feeling in the individual without specific expression in society or one's personal history.

These foundational beliefs do not find their origin or energy in the human soul. Granted that they function outside us in the mind of God, can we conceive that such energy from the divine has no impact on human subjectivity? Must we not believe that the soul created in the image of God, by its very being, participates in the will of God? Would anyone claim that there are no subjective implications for the soul being drawn toward the divine plan through the gracious election of God? Although they may be distorted, do not the hungers, preferences, and tastes of the soul in some way drive it toward its destiny? Is there not a correlation between the providence of God and human hungers and intuitions in the soul?

It is obvious to me that these mighty acts of God in our behalf point toward an inwardness of the will of God. These actions of God in our behalf provide both structure and dynamics for the soul's participation in the will of God. And even admitting the distortions of sin and the impossibility of looking within to inspect the will of God, this faith perspective nevertheless suggests that God's will operates within the human psyche. In some sense it is written into our being.

The Wisdom of the Soul Discovered

Religious thinkers like Augustine have not been the only ones to speculate about the divine purpose's being written into the fabric of the soul. The notion that "something" within the human psyche drives it toward a purpose, toward fulfillment, has been noted by such psychologists as Carl G. Jung, Abraham H. Maslow, and Erik H. Erikson. Although they do not use the language of the Bible, the notion of an internal drive toward wholeness and meaning finds a prominent place at the core of their thinking.

So this disposition of the soul toward fulfillment has not only a transcendent, speculative grounding but also an existential basis. Jung, for example, builds on this predisposition of the psyche in his concept of individuation. According to Jung, all people have within the unconscious dimensions of their being a drive to actualize themselves in certain forms. Jung holds that the psyche has an instinct akin to that of migrating birds or salmon that swim upstream to produce their young. This instinct endeavors to guide the person from within, toward his or her destiny.

No one knew Jung or his thought better than Jolande Jacobi. For many years she worked closely with him, and she interpreted his works in several books. Jacobi offers a summary of Jung's view of individuation: "Taken as a whole, individuation is a spontaneous, natural process within the psyche; it is potentially present in every man [sic], although most men are unaware of it."[2]

Jacobi goes on to describe how this process should occur naturally with one's physical development. But the unfolding of a person's uniqueness can be hampered or blocked. It can also be stimulated and directed by a good therapist who understands the dynamics of human development.

This spontaneous, natural process is an energy that drives the psyche to fulfill its unique reason for being. This instinctual drive toward individuation can be identified as a manifestation of the divine intention operative in the soul, but, though it is present in all people, it can be distorted, obstructed, and inhibited by humanity's bent toward idolatry, substituting "things" for God.

Because Jung considered himself a scientist and did not wish to theologize about the religious nature of the soul, he never articulated this religious connection. But certain of his followers made this and other theological connections. John Sanford, an Episcopal priest and psychoanalyst, expresses this view when he states, "There is something within us that knows who we are and what we are intended to be." The words "something," "who we are," and "who we are supposed to be" stem from the conviction that the divine intention has been written into the psyche.

If this drive can be stimulated, made conscious and elaborated, does this not suggest to a Christian the role of the grace of God? And if one can be helped in this process, does this not call for spiritual guidance?

The notion that the will of God has been stamped in the human psyche finds another expression in the motivational theory of Abraham Maslow. According to Maslow's theory, every person has a drive to satisfy basic human cravings of survival, security, belonging, and selfhood. The drive to meet these needs keeps pressure on the psyche until one need after another finds fulfillment. As lower needs in the hierarchy are met, higher needs become motivating factors. According to Maslow, basic needs provide motivation for actions of the self until satisfied; once these basic needs are met, the person has achieved a freedom that permits him or her to live a self-directed, need-free existence.

Self-actualization, for Maslow, represents being what one is essentially. This essential being is, according to Maslow, written into one's genetic structure. To live in accordance with one's own being issues in wholeness, fulfillment, and the manifestation of higher values. This state of self-actualization is one of "un-needing," in which the psyche does not strive for gratification but expresses its true being freely from within. As an actualizing self, the person no longer lives for need satisfaction but toward the true values of truth, goodness, and beauty.

Is not Maslow describing the dynamic functioning of the

instinct that Jung identifies as directing the psyche toward its individuation? And do not the needs outlined by Maslow define the arena within which the divine will functions? The distinctions between the will of God made flesh in a person and the actualization of the self toward the true, the good, and the beautiful are marginal.

Another psychologist worthy of being cited, Erik Erikson, approaches the phenomenon of the intention within from yet another perspective. Foundational for his discussion of the stages of human development is the epigenetic principle that is derived from the growth of organisms in utero. According to Erikson, "Somewhat generalized, this principle states that anything that grows has a ground plan, and that out of this ground plan the parts arise, each part having its time of special ascendancy, until all parts have arisen to form a functioning whole."[3]

When Erikson refers to the ground plan he points to that genetic coating that actualizes itself first in stages of psychophysical development that govern psychosexual and psychosocial processes. Regarding this process, he says, "At birth the baby leaves the chemical exchange of the womb for the social exchange system of his society, where his gradually increasing capacities meet the opportunities and limitations of his culture."[4]

In the process of physical, sexual, and social evolution, a person passes through a number of crises, forming a unique whole person or failing to form this person. According to Erikson, these crises in development are predictable, and most are age-related. Does not the idea of a ground plan and predictable crises in stages of psychosocial development suggest an inward source of being and life orientation? You can often get a clearer picture of a theorist's ideas by examining the goal toward which he or she moves. Erikson enumerates the attributes of the final stage of development:

> It is the ego's accrued assurance of its proclivity for order and meaning. . . . It is the acceptance of one's one and only life cycle and of the people who have become significant to it as

something that had to be and that, by necessity, permitted of no substitutions . . . a sense of comradeship with men and women of distant times and of different pursuits who created order and objects and sayings conveying human dignity and love.[5]

Does Erikson not underscore the same emphases that we have been asserting about the psyche? Is he not emphasizing the drive in the psyche for order? Does he not border theologically on election and predestination when he suggests the acceptance of one's one and only life as being necessary and permitting no substitutes, as something that had to be? Do not all these assertions point to a ground plan and a directing providence in life?

Yet this discussion of order and purpose cannot proceed without a disclaimer. Although the case has been made for the form of the divine intention written within the human psyche, it does not claim that this intention is unambiguous, obvious, or always attended. Jung would say that the individuation process is blocked by refusing to listen to one's inward dictates. Maslow strives to free a person from the expectations of others and the dictates of culture in order to actualize the unique self. Erickson recognizes that many do not achieve a favorable ratio of the positive and negative elements in the various crises. All the aberrations, stated from a faith perspective, suggest that people neither perceive accurately nor obey perfectly the will of God. In our description of the human situation, we have made it abundantly clear that the "fallen" cannot perceive the divine purpose without the aid of God's Spirit. Yet both the theological and the psychological perspective suggest that something within the psyche has the marking of the divine will and that we do well to attend it.

Perhaps this discussion can return to the place where we began, with Augustine, who said, "Thou hast made us for thyself, O God, and our hearts are restless until they rest in thee." In this affirmation Augustine brings together the two elements of our claim—the theological ("thou hast made us for thyself") and the psychological ("our hearts are restless until they rest in thee").

The reader may be wondering why I would take this treacherous pathway into the human psyche, why I am emphasizing that the will of God may have outlines in the soul. I hope the answer is because it is true. But I would be less than honest if I did not acknowledge my own struggle at this point. Those earliest Christian influences in my life pointed to the will of God as being contained in God's own self or written in the pages of the Bible or spoken by saints past or present. With respect to my own soul, they willingly affirmed that it was so corrupt that nothing of God could possibly come from it; if the will of God did appear to it, my soul could not recognize it. A shorthand summary of this situation might be, "If you think it, if you desire it, if it would be pleasant to you, if you really want to do it, these are evidence enough that it is not of God." This view erases any value that God has given to persons and it places the will of God totally outside the psyche. If this negative perspective is true, how can anyone ever recognize the will of God?

This perversion of the doctrine of sin in humanity obliterates the person, but it also calls into question the notion that we are made in the image of God; that God has loved us so much we have been chosen from the foundation of the world; that a gracious God has intended our lives to be conformed to Christ; and that this gracious, loving God works not only in the depths of the psyche but also in the events of our lives to actualize this divine intention for us.

Capacities of the Soul for Discernment

If we accept the fact that the will of God has been written in the psyche, and if we acknowledge the existential aspects of creation, election, predestination, and providence, we must still inquire into those peculiar capacities of the soul to discern the will of God for a particular individual. With respect to discerning the will of God, the soul has four capacities that require investigation: intuition, imagination, memory, and will. How does reason use these capacities to discern the will of God?

Reason is the human capacity to think, form judgments, and draw conclusions; it is the ability to accumulate, classify, and compare data from which to make choices. This capacity relates to our ability to see, in Christ, the demonstration of the will of God, to say that Christ is the light, the bread, the door, the vine, or the way. To make specific application of this revelation to our concrete situation requires reason. To understand any of the statements of Jesus as they apply to our issues in life requires the use of reason.

But to discern, to judge between what is and what is not God's will, also involves reflection on the data of the inner world. So the data that provide the content of rational thought about the will of God may come through God's revelation in Christ or from the immediate presentation to consciousness from the deeper levels of the self. If the input for reflection appears in consciousness from the outside in the form of the events of our lives, conversations with friends, or the revelation of the will of God in Christ, it also comes from within through intuition, imagination, and memory.

Consider these unique capacities of the psyche, what they are and how they function. Intuition refers to that capacity of the soul to know without rational process. Which of us has not had a sudden flash that revealed to us a pathway to choose or an idea to develop? A friend of mine once remarked that on the very first date he had with his future wife, he knew she was the one he would marry. Often these intuitions come with a conviction that compels action.

Not only does the soul have the capacity to generate intuitions, it also possesses a creative imagination. The imagination functions in conjunction with both intuition and reason. The imagination acts on the data of intuition and reason to visualize concrete enactments of the will of God. Intuition and imagination join in partnership to create new possibilities. So, in discerning the will of God, the intuition may provide impulses, but the creative imagination provides specific expressions of the enactment of the will of God.

For example, suppose a woman has been told by her husband that he wants a divorce. She is discouraged; her work suffers. You know you are to love this person; Christ has commanded it. You see her depth of need for love and affirmation. This "seeing" can be called an intuition. And you picture yourself telling her that God loves her and will sustain her through this crisis. Your imagination visualizes the specific way to express your compassion.

Imagination also functions in memory by reviewing the data of your life to discern the will of God in your personal history. Apart from the creative imagination, the facts of a person's life lie flat, one-dimensional. Without the creative imagination, old interpretations of life remain fixed. The creative imagination provides the leap from facts to meaning— from interpretation to God's intention and from fixed identities to new possibilities. All these functions of the imagination make possible our discernment and actualization of God's will in our history and the projection of that will into the future.

About five years out of seminary I became discouraged. As a young minister, I wondered if I could continue in the ministry. At the time, life seemed dark and unpromising. Yet this crisis opened me to the witness of a friend, it caused me to seek the companionship of zealous Christians, it made me responsive to the challenge of the Holy Spirit, and it gave me courage to try new forms of ministry.

As I review that time in my life, these events are not one-dimensional facts; they are bearers of the will of God for me. I see how they clustered together to give birth to the Lay Witness Mission, a ministry that provided a turning point for me and for numerous others. In "seeing" these meanings my imagination leaps from flat facts to insights into God's activity in my life.

Memory is the capacity to recall past experiences and the interpretation given to them. We weave those interpretations together in the form of a narrative. This narrative, which lies dormant in our memories, is a data base of the activities of God commingled with the struggles of the human spirit to find meaning. At different points in our life journey we have the capacity to recall these experiences and to discern the providences of God in them. Sometimes a shift in perspective enables us to see God's activity which previously had been hidden from view.

The final capacity of the soul to enact the will of God is will, the power of choice. Though the will may not play a major role in discernment prior to our actions, it provides the power to enact it in our lives. Discernment without obedience is an empty exercise.

So these capacities of the soul enable us to reflect on the revelation of God in Christ and on the data from our own soul to discern the divine will. Intuition gives us knowledge of God's will through a nonrational process, imagination enables us to specify new and revived notions that enact the will of God, and will gives us the power to choose what we understand to be God's intention for us. These capacities provide the substance of our exploration of discernment. It would be proper to say that they form elements in the process of knowing anything. And we intend to exploit them for the purpose of knowing the will of God for our lives.

Pitfalls in the Process

Before we begin an investigation of these ways of knowing, we would do well to look at the liabilities that the human psyche as a source of discernment holds. This warning must be issued at the outset to emphasize that the will of God always has a slippery, dual-sided, elusive quality, which demands that we remain open to deeper questions, a clearer vision, and brighter light on our pathway.

Turning to the psyche for clues to the will of God has the drawback of cultural conditioning. All have been nurtured in a particular culture with its codes of right and wrong, its standards, mores, and rituals. Because human beings are, by nature, social, to develop in any other manner would be impossible. Yet the psyche internalizes this cultural umbrella, which casts a shadow under which all discernment is made—and the culture does cast a deep shadow. The skeptic claims that what we call the voice of God is the projection of cultural influences and conditioning.

No doubt cultural conditioning influences the manner and perhaps the context within which we make all discernments. How could it be different? We cannot be stripped of our cultural development and remain human—to be human is to participate in a society and, thus, a culture. From our perspective, God has always made accommodations to the culture. The intention of the divine to become flesh has always meant incarnation in a particular culture—the visible expression of the will of God in a historical setting.

We want to avoid the elevation of any value or norm into competition with God: the deifying of specific expressions of God's will so that they become permanent models and the distortion of God's will as identical with culturally limited perceptions like segregation.

Self-deception should perhaps lead the list of liabilities. Given the condition of human estrangement, we seem to have limitless power for self-delusion; greed and extravagance of the grossest sort can be construed as an evidence of God's blessing; a man may delude himself that he does God's will in exposing the sexual immorality of a brother, when his deeper motives were pride and greed; a woman may claim her personal desires to be synonymous with the will of God. These delusions, and a thousand others, haunt the soul of a serious disciple intent on doing God's will.

Even though the way of discernment faces the peril of self-deception, the only alternatives are agnosticism and indifference. Because serious believers cannot settle for either of these, they willingly risk their own self-deception to claim God's will. We are thankful that we are not left alone in our quest; we have the scriptures, the life and teachings of Jesus, the support of the Christian community, and the gracious providence of God to refine our vision and judge our choices.

Another difficulty in discernment arises from our existential situation. Not only does our cultural conditioning and our vulnerability to self-deception block our discernment; the confusion and general sense of unreality that come in the crises of death, divorce, or any other major change make discernment exceedingly difficult. Trying to see the will of God through the thick cloud of crisis is like looking at the world through

steamed-over glasses. Trauma makes reason difficult; it freezes our intuitions, blocks our imagination, and confuses our
emotions.

In these times, no important decision should be made that
can be avoided. Make the necessary choices and place the others on hold. The intention of God has not excluded us; it has
temporarily gone into eclipse. Batten down the hatches, roll up
the sails, tie the tiller, and ride out the storm.

This inward look at the psyche can produce another problem—an introspective subjectivism. People who are serious
about God's will and sensitive to their own spirits can plunge
so deeply into the inner world of intuition, imagination, and
memory that they get lost. Perhaps this danger caused Jolande
Jacobi to emphasize that the journey was not without peril and
required a companion on the way. "It takes two to undertake
this journey. . . . Any attempt to travel it alone is extremely
dangerous . . . and success is more than doubtful."[6] Even if
people avoid being swallowed by their own unconscious, they
can become so oriented to their inner world that they do not
take seriously the realities of daily life. Such an imbalance
distorts the divine will. As we shall see, the will of God must
never become a matter of speculation separate from concrete
obedience. Safeguards against this perversion lie in balance—a
balance between the inner world of intuition and the outer
world of substantial reality; between individual discernment
and corporate consensus; between the new demands of the
present and the established values of tradition. In addition to
balance, one may also count on an inner wisdom of the soul.
This inner wisdom sounds an alarm when we engage our
own darkness too deeply or when the unconscious makes us
compulsive.

With these pitfalls in mind, we now turn to an investigation of the specific roles of intuition, imagination, and memory
in the work of discernment. After opening the possibilities of
discernment through these internal faculties, we will appeal
to obedient action itself—a balancing factor—as a means of
discernment.

Five

Intuition:
A Source of Discernment

The sign hung across the door, "The Truth Shop." I could hardly believe my eyes, a place to go and purchase the truth.

The saleswoman was quick to respond to my interest: "What kind of truth do you wish, partial or whole?"

"The whole truth, of course, no defenses, no rationalizations, no pretensions." I wanted my truth plain and unadulterated. She motioned me over to the other side of the store.

The salesman in that section pointed to the price tag. "The price is very high, sir," he said.

"What is it?" I asked, determined to get the whole truth, no matter what it cost.

"Your security, sir," he answered.

I came away with a heavy heart.

I wanted both my truth and my safety.

Could I risk the loss of control?[7]

Do we want the truth, the whole truth, the truth that comes from the depth of the soul? And do we dare believe that this mysterious God of creation and providence also speaks through the deep impulses in the soul?

Most of us have so used the power of reason to gain truth

that we have little experience of truth in other forms. Perhaps if we could turn from researcher to poet we would become more competent in the use of intuition, imagination, and memory. Consider the use of intuition in your quest for the meaning of your life. This will require a description of its nature, how it contrasts with rules and dogma, and how it functions in discerning the will of God, plus a few safeguards.

The Meaning of Intuition

The Swiss psychiatrist Carl G. Jung describes four modes of consciousness: sensation, intuition, thinking, and feeling. These modes of awareness identify different ways in which the mind functions. The first two modes indicate the ways we receive data; the latter two, how consciousness acts on these data. Sensation is the capacity to receive data into consciousness by way of the five senses. Intuition is that faculty of the soul by which we receive data from the deeper self. Intuitions come in the form of ideas, hunches, inspirations, and inner vision.

Intuition signifies immediate knowing without the conscious use of reason. A synonym might be instinct, insight, or recognition. Intuition comes from within, from the deeper level of consciousness, the personal unconscious; it functions outside the cause-and-effect relation; it is an autonomous insight that comes with the force of a conviction.

The data of intuition are much like that of an idea; we are stunned when asked, "Where do ideas come from?" A songwriter has a phrase come to mind; it appears from nowhere. Like an idea, it has a spontaneous character. It functions beyond rational control or explanation. Sometimes intuitions come when bidden, but most often they have a timing all their own. Yet there is a convictional quality about insights. They spontaneously erupt from within and grasp reason with a sense of rightness. The correctness of the insight will be strong enough to propel action—even sacrificial action, when the action cannot be justified rationally. Perhaps it is this convictional quality that inspires the courage of a songwriter to express our idea in verse and music. The depth of the idea for the song cannot be denied. Sometimes it seems to have a life of its own.

Intuition has the unique quality of uniting feelings and reason, will and action; in a holistic manner it grasps every facet of our being. Does not intuition, which often comes with a conviction that inspires energy and gives courage, express the soul of the composer?

Intuition seems to have the character of wisdom more than of knowledge. Knowledge is the cognition of facts. Wisdom knows what to do with knowledge: that is, the goal toward which it should move. Maybe wisdom, too, flows from the soul, the depths.

Intuition comes spontaneously from the depths, grasps the whole person, and energizes the will but leaves freedom intact. Were it to be overpowering in effect, it would destroy our human nature. We remain free to choose our own response to a conviction wrought through intuition, even though it is spontaneous, powerful, and convincing. All in all, intuition has the character of a revelation. Like revelation, intuition comes to consciousness, grasps it with its truth, bridges the gap between reason and feeling, and convinces the subject of its validity, while leaving that subject free to choose.

Perhaps a personal experience will illustrate how intuition functions in consciousness. I have said that I went to the desert to pray about the remainder of my life. How the idea for this adventure came to me illustrates the way of intuition. A few years ago my wife, Nan, and I were spending a few days at the beach. I had been quiet and reflective for a day or two. One morning without any premeditation I walked out on the balcony of the condominium and said, "Next year I want to spend a month in the desert." When I heard this statement come from my lips, I think I was as shocked and surprised as Nan was.

The idea of going to the desert for a retreat was new. When I read Carlo Carretto's *Letters from the Desert* I had felt an urge to spend an extended time in solitude. But I had not been thinking about the desert while we were on vacation. The notion came to my mind, and impulsively I spoke it.

In the days that followed, other feelings and ideas began to cluster around this notion. I began to think that at age fifty-five it was too late in life for me to seek approval or recognition. My desire to go to the desert was to be with God because soon I'd be going to God forever and I didn't want to meet God as a stranger. I had an image of entering into a deeper union with God. A hunger to deepen my knowledge of the divine presence gripped my mind.

I began to be aware that these days of solitude would put me in touch with my fear of being alone. For years I had avoided confronting my solitary self for an extended period of time. I had often experienced a one-day silent retreat and on occasions a three-day retreat, but never three or four weeks face to face with myself and God.

Perhaps, too, the desert would afford me a chance to deal with my compulsions. If I became silent enough, long enough, I might encounter the demon that possesses my appetite. Maybe through prayer and fasting even this one would be cast out. These reflections illustrate the ideas that clustered about the original idea.

I cannot explain the power of this intuition to go to the desert. Almost every day for a year I thought it. The idea of the solitude created a deep hunger, even a longing, in me. My internal responses both of thought and feeling felt strange. I, who had always been afraid of loneliness and inactivity—this extroverted person was actually looking forward to the desert!

I began to feel that the time set apart was for "listening to God," for discerning what I was to do with the last third of my life. Something within seemed to tell me I would not be the same after this experience; it would be a watershed in my life. One day I was reading over some notes in my journal about this experience and I came across this statement: "I feel that what I have written about the desert is a prophecy as well as a deep desire within me."

This intuition regarding the desert has been an element in my discerning the will of God for my life. It may have much in common with all intuitions, but there was something about this urge to go to the desert that seemed to me distinctly spiritual and Christian. My intuition had a kinship to the songwriter's inspiration—spontaneity and immediacy; it had a sense of rightness about it and a conviction strong enough to propel action. This sudden insight grasped both feelings and will and had the character of wisdom.

Probably any creative idea, whether or not consciously identified with Christ, would have many of these characteristics. What made this intuition different for me lay in its revelational and convictional nature. As I reflected on the experience, the notion of going to the desert had a numinous quality, a sense of the holy in it. The thought inspired a mixture of reverence, awe, and wonder. It seemed God had revealed to me what I was to do, with conviction enough to cause me to do it. Yet in this experience I did not forfeit freedom. The choice to go always seemed to be my own.

Although intuition is not the only entrée God has to us, it provides a helpful means for discovering the will of God for our lives. By no means do all intuitions present to us the will of God—far from it. But some intuitions present us with notions that do have a convictional or revelational nature, a feeling that gives hints of the divine. In the power of human freedom, we must distinguish the will of God from our own will or some alien will.

Whereas this illustration focuses on the dedication of my life, we may have intuitions about all kinds of issues—from work to marriage to children to human relations—and the inner wisdom of the soul comes to us to direct and guide our lives. I am convinced that intuitions do at times present the will of God to us. Discernment must determine whether intuitions are of God or of ourselves. My intuition about the desert, I came to believe, revealed the will of God to me.

How is the presence of God related to intuition? In this regard, I have been influenced by Jung's view of the soul as having three dimensions: consciousness, the personal unconscious, and the collective unconscious. The collective unconscious, for Jung, is the racial memory, and through this racial memory the entire experience of the human race impinges on each individual soul. The personal unconscious contains repressed material (à la Freud), but it also stores the vast, untapped potential of the individual. The drive toward individuation lies in the unconscious, as does the ground plan of our lives. Personal consciousness provides the meeting ground between inner and outer worlds.

This view of the soul suggests that God comes to us from the outside through sensation (that is, the use of the five senses) and from the inside through intuition. Later we will have more to say about God's encounter with us through our history and through the current events of our lives, but at this point we will inquire more pointedly about the revelation of God from within.

I visualize, beneath the collective unconscious (the racial memory), the memory of God. All that has been since the dawn of creation resides in the memory of God. But woven through that memory is God's will for all creation, for all of human history. And this will is not a dead, lifeless entity. Rather, it is powerful, active, energizing, and personal. This omnipotent, loving presence, in the form of a will, impinges on the personal unconscious of every human being. In both its subtlety and its graciousness, it touches the personal unconscious and stimulates images of the divine will that erupt into consciousness as intuitions. Perhaps the wisdom conveyed in our intuitions arises from the racial memory and the personal history, plus the divine initiative.

In asserting that the divine will comes to us through our intuition, I am by no means suggesting that every intuition of the soul expresses the will of God. Other forces certainly inspire our intuitions. Morton Kelsey, as well as Scott Peck, would say that the personal unconscious is exposed to the demonic as well as the divine. We should also expect an influence on intuitions from the repression of negative data, the dark side of our personality, and perhaps even the racial memory. These possibilities all point to the issue that concerns us here—the necessity of discerning the voice of God in the intuitions of the soul.

Contrasting Approaches to God's Will

I have indicated in the definition of sensation and intuition that the will of God may come from without or within. In contrast to intuition, the will of God may come through providence and tradition and through rules or regulations. For most people, guidance through tradition or rules has been the first and most trusted way of direction.

It is easy to see why external guidance prevails. As children we were reared in a culture that established norms for behavior. Because the culture of our youth came from adults, the norms seemed to have a divine sanction. The values our parents taught us became synonymous with God's will. Therefore, we acquired notions such as God wills us to work hard, be honest, save money. It is not God's will for us to be lazy, inconsiderate, or sexually promiscuous. These rules for life found a place in our souls before we had the power of reason or the ability to discern for ourselves.

This approach to God's will has the strength of tradition behind it; it has been refined through the ages. Because this culture has been tested through the generations, it tends to generate greater trust. As a consequence we look outside ourselves to cultural rules to discern the will of God.

As valuable and trustworthy as rules may be, they have certain weaknesses, limitations, and inadequacies. The rules do not always fit the specific situation. When, for example, a daughter has a normal, loving relationship with her parents, the external command to honor her father and mother fits. But suppose another daughter has been abused by her father and not been trusted by her mother. How can "Honor your father and mother" have the same meaning as for a daughter affirmed by her father and loved by her mother? In the instance of abuse, what standard offers the daughter guidance?

Dependence on rules for guidance has another limitation. Rules always speak in general categories, not in specific instances. The tradition says that a man should take a wife, legitimizing the institution of marriage. But it does not tell the man which woman he should choose. Thus both the man and the woman are left with the culturally sanctioned choice of a mate, but with the responsibility and freedom to discern who that mate will be. How does a person discern the specific person he or she is to marry?

There remains still another inadequacy of depending on cultural rule for guidance—the gap between the rules and individual affections. There are instances in which the rules may be known in the mind, without eliciting the affections of the heart. A youngster was told by his mother to stand when his grandmother came into the room. When his mother insisted on this polite behavior, he said, "When she comes into the room I may be standing in my posture, but in my heart I'll be sitting down."

This estrangement of affection and will introduces innumerable problems relating to human rebellion and the divine will. Yet I introduce this contradiction to make a single point: "God does not desire reluctant obedience." God desires an obedience that finds expression not only in the hand or foot but also in the heart.

Guidance from within, through intuition, can bridge divisions that guidance through rules cannot. Perhaps the intuition complements the generalized rules that embody the will of God. In most instances intuitions arise in the midst of a life situation; they are colored by life experience. The abused daughter who has come to know Christ brings to the command "Honor your father and mother" the pain of rejection and injury mixed with God's acceptance and forgiveness. Cannot the intuitions regarding parental respect that arise from her faith be trusted?

With respect to the general institution of marriage, the intuition particularizes this divine intention: this is the man; this is the woman. In most instances the courage to marry a particular person depends on a strong intuition that he or she is the right person.

Intuition grasps the whole person. Because of this power, our intuitions have the power to unite the will and the affections. In my experience of being called to the desert, I faced a number of ambiguous feelings. On the one side, I felt the call of God; on the other, the fear of loneliness. Yet the intuition regarding God's will was strong enough to unite my feelings with my will.

Attention to one's intuition adds the dimension of excitement to the life with God. The religious life for some has been dull, monotonous, routine. The devout life has seemed more like obeying laws or meticulously following a road map than like the adventure of an explorer blazing a new trail. Attention to one's intuition also adds a spontaneous, unpredictable excitement to finding God's will.

Yet the way of discernment through intuition is exposed to danger. To travel this road incurs risk. We risk the loss of control through the eruption of truth so powerful that it demands a response of obedience. Sometimes this risk is heightened, when decisions reach beyond catechism and code, and demand responses where scripture has no voice.

The Way of Intuition

Can intuition help a person discern God's will? How can a power so uncontrollable and unpredictable become a source for discerning something so holy and sublime as the will of God? There are at least five ways that intuition aids us. It provides alternative images of the future, gives a sense of the situation, helps resolve conflicting feelings, assesses character in relationships, and furnishes creativity.

A closer look at the functions may be of help in making decisions: for example, a promotion and geographical move. Intuition assists us in deciding a course of action by providing alternative images of the future. In this instance intuition operates in the present but provides images that are future. When, for example, a career choice must be made, the intuition provides images of the new career, as if it were an accomplished fact. The intuition generates images of what it will be like in the new position, in a new location, with a different group of people. These images have either a magnetic, alluring quality or no attraction at all. Those images that create a conviction within us, a sense that this is both what we want and what we should do, may be the images inspired by the Spirit of God. If these images have a strong convictional quality, they should give us pause.

Intuition, then, provides the sense of a situation, a feeling of rightness or caution. After you have investigated the opportunity for advancement, examining both the pros and the cons, the intuition usually provides you a sense of the rightness of the move. I cannot say this sense of rightness always expresses the will of God. Other factors must be considered. But the intuition in its suprarational perception of truth often "knows" the appropriate choice for you to make. If you do not have an intuitive sense of rightness about a proposed course of action, you should delay the decision.

The intuition also functions to resolve conflict in our relationships and in our personality. Our intuition has a type of autonomy that shatters an established mind-set, sometimes an illusory one. Suppose the man who has been given a chance for a promotion that involves moving to another city actually goes to that city to investigate the job and the community. For some time he has had an obsession with his wife's unfaithfulness. In his rational moments he knows that she is a "one-man woman." Nevertheless, when he travels out of town a neurotic fear of his wife's unfaithfulness possesses him. Even though he knows the illusory nature of this fear, it grasps him on occasion with a demonic force.

When he goes to investigate the new position, he finds himself checking into a hotel room in a city far from home. While signing his credit card form, he notes a beautiful woman who is also checking in. Amazingly, the same porter takes their luggage to the seventh floor. Her room is located right next to his. That evening after dinner he is overcome with the notion that the woman next door has amorous feelings for him. His fantasy becomes wild with images of encounter and lovemaking.

Then, to his utter surprise, an idea erupts in his consciousness: "You are the person capable of being unfaithful, not your wife." That insight enables him to own the dark side of himself, and after the confession of his own tendency toward lust and evil imaginations he is no longer gripped with the paranoia regarding his wife. An insight that came to him as an intuition has revealed the nature of his neurotic obsession and liberated him from it.

Intuitions often hint at the character of another person. These impressions, which cannot be fully described, should never be taken as absolute truth, but they cannot be denied either. For example, when this man who is responding to the company's offer of a promotion meets the woman who will be his boss in the new town, she will have spontaneous impressions of him. All the data look good—strong academics, several years' experience in the field, references stating "intelligent, creative, industrious, likable, easy to get along with"—but during the interview her intuition picks up static. Something inside tells her that this is not the man. Reason points toward transferring him, but intuition speaks a different message. She will ignore her intuition to her own detriment.

Some people do not have as strong intuitions as others, or they do not trust them or are not as sensitive to them. These people tend to trust the data of their senses more than their intuitions. One of my friends has a highly developed sensory system; he has used it successfully to expand a small family corporation into operations in more than twenty countries. He does not lack intelligence, but when he hires a new top-level officer for the company he arranges for the prospective employee and his or her spouse to have dinner with him and his wife. Through the years he has learned that his wife has a strong, intuitive perception. On more than one occasion he has disregarded her intuition about a prospective employee to his later dismay. Now he arranges the dinner engagement to give her a chance to size up the situation.

This intuitive sense of another cannot always be stated; it may be more of a feeling. In search of God's will, this function of the intuition has implications for mates as well as for employees, for friends and others with whom we share responsibility.

Intuition also relates to creativity. An idea pops into a person's head, identifying a task, a style, or a method of doing a job. The subject does not know where the idea arises, but it comes with such conviction that it cannot easily be resisted; nor can it be ignored because it returns again and again. Each response to the notion tends only to intensify and expand it.

I can illustrate this idea with the book you are reading. One afternoon I visited with my pastor in his office. During the conversation he mentioned two books I had written, *To Will God's Will* and *To Pray God's Will.* Hearing these two titles evoked an idea. "A sequel to these two books needs to be written—*To Find God's Will.*" The idea came unbidden; it grasped me with a deeper and deeper conviction. Although I had two other books in mind at the time, the idea of "discerning God's will" displaced them. With one line of a book, the title, I began opening myself to the idea. Almost every day for a month I identified basic ideas suggested by the title and the points that clustered around these notions. Soon I had twenty-five pages of notes. They lay on my table like clay waiting to be shaped by a potter.

When this kind of creative intuition occurs, I find that it takes up residence in my mind; I seem to think about it throughout the day. An idea of this caliber possesses that convictional quality that will not let me get away from it. It also exerts a kind of seduction that allures my soul, a draw that simultaneously teases, excites, and beckons. In this way, intuition creates a collection of ideas and images.

I had this same repetition of an idea when I had the intuition to spend time in the desert. The intuition came the latter part of May. It returned with greater conviction and enlarged possibilities over the next few weeks. Each time it came it presented itself with greater clarity and a deeper feeling of rightness. I began to respond to the idea and to make plans for the journey. Each day for an entire year I thought about the journey to the desert and what it meant for my life.

I have given some different examples of how the intuition works in discernment. Keep in mind, however, that intuitions must not be uncritically identified with God's will. They are but one medium revealing God's intention for us, and they must be judged using Christ as the norm for discerning God's will.

I had finished an hour's discussion of intuition as a means

of discernment when one of the students asked, "How do we stimulate our intuitions?" The question is a legitimate one but not so easy to answer. Our best intuitions seem to come when we have some distance between ourselves and the issues, or when we have made a major shift in vocation or residence, or when we are "looking the other way." Often our best intuitions come when we least expect them. Whenever or however they do come, be prepared to jot them down for reflection later.

I explained to my inquirer and to the class that intuitions cannot be compelled by human desire, yet certain environments seem to spawn them. In silence the complex mystery of our being often speaks to us through images that arise from the unconscious. Yet do not claim that God has spoken the final word to you. (See the exercise for chapter 5 in Appendix A for guidance in creating an environment for the intuitions.)

The Slippery Road of Intuitions

When I use the metaphor of the slippery road to describe intuitions, I have in mind a drive from a small monastery tucked away in a canyon on the Chama River some thirteen miles from a paved road. The guest master warned me that if it rained, even lightly, the clay would become slick as glass. It did rain and because of personal pressures, I set out in a '76 Chevy to find a phone. After spinning and sliding, narrowly missing a crash over the precipice of a canyon wall, passing some cars in the ditch and others turning back, in an hour and three quarters I traversed the thirteen-mile stretch. Sometimes I think intuitions are almost as treacherous as that thirteen miles of road. How dependable are they as revelations of God's will, and how should they be dealt with?

All of us have intuitions. They come to us in the ways and with the force I have described. Although intuitions are sources of guidance, three cautions should be sounded.

First, do not become captive to your intuitions. That is, accept uncritically the inspirations of the deeper self. All knowledge that comes by intuition should be tested by reason. "Does it makes sense?" we should ask.

Second, remember that your intuitions are filtered through your social and psychological history. They are never "the pure voice of God" but always have a certain dissonance caused by our historical experiences that defuse and distort the revelation of God. In walking this slippery road of intuition, never forget the capacity of the soul for self-delusion. You and I, all of us, have an uncanny ability to convince ourselves that what we desire is what God desires for us. Don't reject an intuition because it expresses a deep desire of your own, but do not uncritically embrace it either. Keep asking the question, "Is this intuition what Christ wills for me?"

Finally, the data of the intuition must be laid on the transparent Christ. Does it coincide with the revelation we have discovered in the incarnate God? If it contradicts the example and teaching of Christ, it cannot be God's will. If it expresses the mind and spirit of Christ, the intention is probably, but not necessarily, of God.

Having looked at the role of intuition in discerning the will of God, we now ask how the creative imagination can give fuller shape to the intention of God for our lives.

Six

Imagination and Discernment

Does it shock you that I would point to the imagination as a faculty of discernment? Imagination, at first glance, suggests child's play, unreality, the world of fantasy. Can this world so closely related to that slippery world of illusion actually unfold a vision of reality—ultimate reality, the will of God?

In how many ways has imagination gone wild? Immediately I think of the child who in the night hears the tramp of Bigfoot; the mental patient who imagines she is Joan of Arc, or the Virgin Mary; the feigned paralysis of the neurotic, in whom the imagination has been taken captive by the dark side of the unconscious, or the hallucinations of the psychotic who sees visions of extraterrestrials.

How could I place the discernment of the will of God in company with these untamed, if not bizarre, products of the imagination? Can the imagination be subdued and made to serve the deeper needs of the soul and the purposes of God?

A further examination of the imagination suggests a deeper meaning. Rather than a partner in illusion, imagination constructs reality by forming images of what is not immediately present and by creating visions of new possibilities. The imagi-

nation manifests a powerful creative faculty to compose, de-
compose, and recompose the meaning of our lives.

Perhaps a narrative will underscore the power of imagination to create meaning in a person's life. I first met Ann Dailey
(not her real name) when I was preaching in the church she
attends. She told me an amazing story that illustrates the power
of imagination in the creation of meaning.

The crucial day was December 9, 1986; the place, the
Academy Theatre. She had gone to the theater to see a rec-
ommended play, *The People of the Brick,* a depiction of the life
of the homeless in her city. The unique feature of this production was that the actors were truly homeless people who,
after each evening's production, went back to the street for
the night.

On that fateful day, Ann Dailey went home after the play,
crawled between fresh, warm sheets, and tried to go to sleep.
But sleep escaped her. She lay there in the safety of her apartment contrasting her life with the lives of hundreds of people
on the street that very night.

With a shocked awareness, the idea came to her that she
could do something about the plight of street people. Her
imagination began to churn out images of how she could make
a difference in their lives. Like fragments of a vision the ideas
began to fall into place:

> I have more than I need.
> I have $1,000 in cash.
> I want to help.
> With some of my own furnishings I can create a few home kits—a
>   fork, a plate, a cup, a cloth to wash with.
> A few dollars for part of a month's rent.

And thus the vision grew as she let her imagination loose.

As Ann told me about this experience, her mind seemed
to return to that night. There had been nothing special about
the evening, no feeling of destiny in going to the play, no
special sense of need to do anything for anyone. She looked
calm and relaxed as she recalled being confronted by the vision
of a new and different future for herself.

"How strange, how strange indeed, for me to find myself in such a role. It's the last thing I would have ever dreamed of," she said. Then she began to rehearse how she had been reared in that church and, as a child, sang in the choir. During her college days she had forgotten about church; then she got married and suffered six years of battering before she got a divorce. After the divorce her life had been less than "disciplined"; she spent her nights in bars and had an assortment of boyfriends. She became pregnant, gave birth to a daughter, overcame alcoholism, and set up a business in her home. Hers was the story of a woman whose life had been distorted and confused.

As she thought back to December 9, 1986, she recalled, "I had felt so sorry for myself until that night, and after the play I lay there in bed comparing my life with that of those four people I had seen on the stage. Suddenly, I saw something that I could do to make a difference in the world.

"I finally allowed myself to be touched. Through my struggles I had allowed myself to become bitter and angry, but God had been working in my life without my even knowing it."

Somehow, in listening, I knew that life was much better for Ann now. She had purpose. She had a sense of God.

Then she confirmed my intuitions: "Now I have such peace and joy. I am rich. I love the people with whom I work. I love my work. Life is truly an adventure."

Ann has continued her work with the homeless. She fulfills the demands of a regular job, and with the aid of church members and a few friends she helps homeless people get off the street and into their own dwellings. Her life continues to blossom with meaning and a rich witness for Christ.

Ann's story enables us to look more closely at the positive use of the imagination. The imagination can bring into the present what is buried in memory, like the images of God and the experiences of church from other years; it can re-create an image of a person not present or an event that occurred in the past. This faculty, gone wild, hears voices, sees visions of monsters, and suffers the terrors of the dark side associated with demons and ghosts. But this same faculty, brought under control and disciplined, also has the power to make us aware of Christ and his presence in our lives today.

In George Bernard Shaw's play *Joan of Arc,* Joan declares that she hears the voice of God. Her critics tell her that the voices come from her imagination, to which Joan retorts, "Of course, that is how the messages of God come to us."[8]

Our examination of the Fourth Gospel as the record of an incarnation of the will of God lies dead or is reduced to a new law apart from the power of a creative imagination. Surely it is the creative imagination that projects us, here and now, into the presence of Christ. As Jesus speaks to the woman taken in adultery, "Neither do I condemn you. Go, and sin no more," he speaks the same message to us: "Neither do I condemn *you.* Go, and sin no more." To hear the word of God in our personal, contemporary circumstance requires the creative work of the imagination.

In some fashion did this not happen to Ann when she was grasped with the conviction that her life could make a difference in the world? Was Christ not present to her in that moment?

The imagination not only resurrects history stored in memory, it also constructs new possibilities. Undisciplined by a neurotic mind, the imagination pictures such catastrophes as bankruptcy, a wife that does not return, dead children beside a wreck on the highway. But, disciplined, the imagination can expand an intuition into a vision of the future or see new possibilities never before imagined.

When I write a book, for example, I can envision the project completed, the book published, and the reader absorbing the ideas and sharing the experiences. The imagination creates images, making the future become present. Imagination takes the form of God's will, gives it specific content, and envisions its consequences, though never fully or clearly.

Imagination also can leap from images, data, or flat experience to meaning and purpose. The data of experience come to us without name or significance: that is, without interpretation. And the imagination, grasping and acting on the facts of experience, squeezes meaning from the actualities. Did not this happen for Ann as her imagination moved, from the actors in the play, first to herself and then to a new future for both her and them?

The hunger for meaning seems so basic to human beings that we might even call it an instinct, but the meaning sought does not come neatly wrapped and tied with a ribbon. Whatever meaning comes to us arrives in the raw data of experience. And usually in retrospect, as the data are reviewed, the imagination derives its meaning. Even as you experience those seminal events in your own life, the imagination hovers over these occurrences and creates meaning while connecting them with the evolving narrative of your life.

We have said that the human hunger for meaning finds its ultimate satisfaction in the will of God. Thus the imagination engages in the task of reading or discerning the will of God in the events of a particular life. For example, a minister receives a call to a particular congregation. The call provides new opportunities and challenges. The imagination translates the data of the call into an ongoing narrative of the minister's life. With what might be called a "second vision," the imagination also perceives the hand of God at work in the events.

While serving in a new parish, an innovative minister develops a special ministry to retired persons. Her spiritual development program receives national attention, and she is invited to give leadership in forming a national program for her denomination. In retrospect, it seems clear that God placed her in that retirement community, provided months of struggle, energy, and creativity, and then slowly guided her into this new ministry. This vision and interpretation of her life depends on the power of a disciplined imagination—the capacity to leap from the facts of experience to their interpretation and meaning.

The imagination also has the capacity to make creative applications of insights; to see, for example, the will of God in one context and transfer that vision to a different situation. The effective interpretation of scripture always requires this type of transfer. In biblical interpretation, two questions must always be answered: What does the text say? What does it mean to us? The creative application occurs between the "say" and the "mean."

Consider the biblical text, for example, which describes Peter's rooftop vision at Simon the tanner's in Joppa:

> The next day, as they were on their way and coming near Joppa, Peter went up on the roof of the house about noon in order to pray. He became hungry, and wanted to eat; while the food was being prepared he had a vision. He saw heaven opened and something coming down that looked like a large sheet being lowered by its four corners to the earth. In it were all kinds of animals, reptiles, and wild birds. A voice said to him, "Get up, Peter; kill and eat!"
>
> But Peter said, "Certainly not, Lord! I have never eaten anything ritually unclean or defiled."
>
> The voice spoke to him again, "Do not consider anything unclean that God has declared clean." This happened three times, and then the thing was taken back up into heaven.
>
> (Acts 10:9–16, TEV)

The text says that Peter had a vision of a sheet filled with unclean meats (for a Jew). He was told to kill and eat. Peter refused but was told not to consider unclean the thing that God had cleansed.

When the visitors arrived from Cornelius to tell Peter of their master's vision, Peter understood the vision. The Gentiles were not unclean. Thus we see how Peter's imagination enabled him to move from vision to meaning. But how do we move from the story of Peter to meaning in our own lives?

Pondering this text, one student "saw" that the shattering of Peter's cultural conditioning with respect to the uncleanness of the Gentiles spoke to him regarding his attitudes toward gays and lesbians. Homophobia was as much a part of his heritage as estrangement from the Gentiles was part of Peter's heritage. This application of the biblical text occurred through a powerful imagination capable of transferring the meaning from one setting to another.

This interpretative role of the imagination becomes critical whenever we ask how a particular idea or behavior compares with the biblical norm of the revelation of God in Christ. Christ has revealed that we are to love and serve one another, that we are to be one, but we must turn to our creative imagination to give specific focus and content to the divine will in a particular situation. Without the power of a creative imagination the will of God remains a noble ideal, expressed in sacred texts but not incarnate in the lives of contemporary believers.

The imagination has one other function in the lives of those who seek God's will; it re-creates. Recall how Ann's life was re-created by the Spirit through her imagination! She had turned inward, become bitter, and life had little meaning for her. With this newly created life she was filled with peace and joy and had a deep sense of purpose in her life. This recomposing has three applications: when a life finds a new sense of meaning; when a structured life has been shattered by death, moral failure, or catastrophe; and when a life's meaning has been built on a false foundation and has become pointless or stuck. In each of these instances, life no longer has meaning; it has lost its reason for being or, as in the instance of conversion, has discovered a new reason for being.

Reason fulfills the role of analysis—what happened? Why did it happen? What options are available? The data produced by these questions provide the substance over which imagination broods to construct new meaning.

The ambiguity of life, the perverseness of the human heart, and the consequences of both ambiguity and perverseness make the constructive power of imagination play a crucial role in discerning the will of God. When life has been shattered through the death of a mate and meaning evaporates, forcing the will of God into an eclipse, slowly and tentatively the imagination reconstructs a new vision of the future and begins to identify God's will in the ongoing events of life.

When life gets stuck through resistance to one's true self or from building on a faulty foundation, reason analyzes but imagination reconstructs. In this reconstructive process God comes to us with a fresh revelation of the divine will. Perhaps patience is the virtue most needed.

The new center of meaning, from a spiritual perspective,

is often an experience of conversion, the revelation of a new truth, or the birth of a new relationship. In these instances the changes are as radical as those that have negative causes. The new center, although a gracious bestowal of God's self, grasps human consciousness with such power that the perception and direction of one's life must change. As the presence of God explodes in a life, the creative imagination must again reimage the identity and life-style of the person.

How shall we summarize what we have been discovering about the role of imagination in discerning the will of God? Perhaps another illustration will show more clearly how it functions in forming the will of God in our minds. In discussing intuition I spoke about the call to go to the desert and the focus on discerning God's will for the remainder of my life. When I got to the little monastery, Christ in the Desert, my chief task was to seek God's will for the remaining one third of my life.

I resolved to attend each of the offices (time of prayer centered in the psalms), and the first office, vigils, began at 4:00 A.M. This corporate prayer of the community seemed to form a spiritual womb in which I could attend to the task for which I had come.

My second day at the monastery I began a review of my life. I divided it into five-year intervals, focused on those years, and wrote down the images that flooded my mind. After finishing each period of my life, I listed the dominant themes during those five years. I spent two days reflecting in this manner on my history.

With this renewed awareness of my history and the themes that had dominated my life, I began to think about the future in five-year blocks. Beginning with the fifty-five-to-sixty segment, I thought about the significant people in my life, the changes taking place in my body, and the sense of God's call. Against this background I brooded over what I should be doing with my life in each period. All the ideas that came to consciousness, I wrote down.

I continued this process of creative imaging in five-year increments until my eighty-fifth year. In each period I tried to visualize where I would be, whom I would be associated with, how my time would be invested, what losses I would suffer, and how I would seek to glorify God.

I spent the better part of four days imaging the future. On Sunday—it happened to be Pentecost Sunday—I envisioned my own death. This whole imaginative adventure may seem presumptuous to some people, depressing to others, and perhaps vain to yet others. Whatever evaluation other people may make, I found it most helpful to think through my life. We have two options: we can anticipate our future or we can ignore it.

At age fifty-five I thought it was too late for triviality. I had twenty or twenty-five years left to accomplish what God placed me on this earth to do. I did not want to waste the time God had given me.

I hope this experience will give you an idea about the use of your creative imagination in reviewing your history, in creating new possibilities for the future, in interpreting your experiences, and in making creative applications of God's will to your particular circumstances. You can use this approach to imagination in dealing with a single issue or a whole life issue.

Destructive Use of the Imagination

Thus far we have alluded to the negative possibilities of the imagination as childish fantasy, severed from reality, but most of our reasoning has sought to justify the creative and constructive use of the imagination in discerning God's will. Yet honesty demands that we examine the negative ways in which imagination can function to blur, diffuse, disguise, and destroy perceptions of God's will. Often the pathway between the creative and chaotic functions of imagination narrows perilously, and a misstep can spell pain and loss.

At the outset we have acknowledged that the human creature is not today what God had originally intended. Something has occurred that severed human consciousness from direct and sustained intercourse with God. For this reason the imagination does not always function in accord with the divine intention; it can even act to pervert God's will and destroy meaning.

Still another factor makes imagination suspect. In addition

to the loss of divine immediacy, there seem to be alien forces that impinge on the imagination with destructive consequences. Whether these negative influences arise from the general forces of evil or the negative aspects of the human personality, we cannot say for sure. One fact we can declare: "Something" acts on the imagination, causing it to produce negative, erroneous visions of reality. The perverted imagination shows itself in our self-rejection, fears, suspicions, and despair. All these perversions distort our discernment of the will of God.

Alien powers, whether demons, repressed guilt, or estranged human nature, cause the imagination to create self-hate and images of an unacceptable self. Perhaps these alien powers arise from the negative images buried in memory, images of the self as inadequate, incompetent, and inferior. This negative self-perception screens out the love of God and the awareness of God's purpose, much as tanning lotion screens out the sun's ultraviolet rays.

A hundred sources could have triggered the original negation of the self created in the image of God: for example, lack of parental love, negative comparisons with a sibling, failure to measure up to one's own or one's parents' expectations, or a moral failure. At the time of these occurrences the imagination, in a flash, judged the self guilty and unacceptable. This rash conclusion may have originally included significant others and one's self and later expanded to include God.

As long as this person remains captive to the negative imagination, it blocks the awareness of the love of God. "If God does not love me," the soul reasons, "how could God have a purpose for my life?" The conception of a worthless self and the unconditional love of God seem to me mutually exclusive. If God loves you, you have value. Fortunately the sense of worthlessness and self-hate is not absolute, and most people who are plagued by these negative imaginations possess a mixture of self-acceptance and self-rejection.

To the extent that we discount our worth as creations of God, we erect barriers to the divine will. On the other hand, when the imagination can envision a self created by God, loved by God, and included in the ultimate intention of the Creator, space is created to experience the will of God. The conviction that we, although sinners, are freely justified by Christ liberates us from these destructive, negative illusions about ourselves.

The imagination also acts destructively in the creation of unreal fears. The imagination in the power of our unconscious flashes negative pictures into our conscious minds: exposures that never happen, rejections we never experience, catastrophes that do not occur, isolation and loneliness that never come. These unreal fears arise from spurious creations of the imagination.

Could it be the will of a gracious God to injure those who bear the divine image? As in the case of self-hate, we cannot simultaneously foster images of fear and the unconditional love of God. Fears diminish immediately in the presence of God's love. Even if occurrences threaten us, we can face these changes through God's will.

Self-hate points to negative imaginings in the past that distort our perception in the present. Unreal fears point to negative imaginings of the future that blind us to the will of God in the present. And suspicions block us from a positive relationship with a brother or a sister here and now. Suspicion is fear turned toward another.

We have shown that intuition furnishes us with perceptions of new people we meet, as well as with perceptions of those who are regularly in our lives. Although intuitions may not hold up under the test of a deepened relation, they often prove true. A destructive imagination takes the intuition of another's weakness and turns it into a suspicion. Suspicions usually turn back on the person who holds them. They are seen as the other person's intentions to cheat, destroy, or do us in

But God wills us to love the neighbor. Love and suspicion contradict each other. Suspicion is fear of the other, and love casts out fear. We are not suggesting a naïve, face-value acceptance of every person who enters our lives. Such an uncritical embrace would make us too vulnerable. Yet we must cast down negative images that have been inspired and built up by a perverse imagination.

The final issue caused by the negative imagination is despair. If fear suggests the creation of a negative future, despair implies the loss of a future. In this regard the imagination is not negative but paralyzed. Despair results from the imagination's inability to create a future. When the imagination becomes impotent, it says to the soul, "You have no future."

If there is no future, there can be no meaning, no purpose, no hope. Without a future, there can be no meaning attached to the will of God. The "nothingness" of the future contradicts the power and purposiveness of the Creator. God said and ever says, "Let there be."

In moments or seasons of despair, we must not run away from our emptiness. Neither should we succumb to the fear of an empty future. As difficult as it may seem, we must embrace our despair, take it into ourselves with patience, and wait for the awakening of our imagination, which then can create a positive future. In other words, we must wait until hope is born. Hope opens the door for the reappearance of the will of God into our consciousness.

Is it not becoming clear to us that the creative imagination has amazing power to construct meaning in our lives: that is, to provide concrete choices to actualize the will of God? And is it not equally clear that the negative imagination can block our perception of God's intention as it appeared in the past, as it meets us in the present, as it challenges us in all our relationships, and as it would guide us toward our destiny? Between the constructive and the destructive potential of the imagination, human life in search of God's will must be lived. This "land between" points toward life lived neither in the blissful certainty that all actions accord with God's will nor in the destructive despair that nothing we ever do pleases God. I am pointing to a yes-and-no in the disciple's life, the land of ambiguity in which we both actualize and deny the will of God; this tension creates the situation of "being and not being" in the will of God.

The Will of God and Our Ambiguous Embodiments

To say that the will of God may be discussed and fulfilled ambiguously may raise unanswered questions. The word "ambiguity" is not too common in our speech. What do we mean by the phrase "living in ambiguity"? To illustrate ambiguity, we might think of the congruence of a star and a circle. Because fundamental differences exist in these two shapes, they can never be completely congruent. But if they have similar diameters, the two figures will have an approximate congruency. We fulfill the will of God with the approximation of the star/circle congruence.

The reasons for this ambiguity arise from our lack of clear perception, our inadequate translation of perceived behavior, and our sinfulness. The most generalized way of describing the source of this ambiguity is to point to "fallen" human nature. Because of the Fall, we human beings no longer possess an immediate intuition of the divine will, nor do we have a fully functioning imagination constructive of a vision of God's will; human volition also lacks a freedom to enact the divine intention.

I see this ambiguity in all the functions of the imagination. If the imagination functions ambiguously, then discernment of God's will is also ambiguous. For example, imaging the past can only be done imperfectly, thus ambiguously. So to image Christ in the present, to discern the meaning of his words in the contemporary world, can never be absolute.

In the parable of the good Samaritan, Jesus teaches the crucible of love and service. But how we express this love in concrete situations will always have limits. Each act of love and service will be ambiguous because of the imperfection of discernment and obedience.

The same logic holds true regarding a vision of the future. Abram was certain of God's call, and the promise of the divine pointed clearly into the future. But Abram's perception of that will often seemed vague and inexact, not to mention the imperfection of his obedience. Beside the daring faith with which he led Isaac up the mountain to be sacrificed, we place his lack of trust in God when he had a son from Hagar. He also lied to the pharaoh, claiming that his wife was his sister. Such is the ambiguity and perversion of the imagination darkened by sin.

In the construction of purpose from the raw data of experience we also meet ambiguity. From the data of Saul's conversion and courageous witness, Barnabas recognized a special purpose at work in the soul. Thus when Barnabas was sent to Antioch to teach for a year (Acts 11), he first went to Tarsus in search of Saul. Even though this partnership would eventually fail, the sensitive discernment and courageous response of Barnabas proved a decisive factor in Saul's life.

All the other functions of the imagination—new creations and recompositions of old ones—suffer the same ambiguous consequences we have described. Do the inadequacies of our discernment and reconstruction through the creative imagination lead us to despair? By no means! The recognition of the ambiguity of discernment saves us from both pride and dogmatism. As proof of this assertion, I ask you only to recall the person in your life who has no awareness of his or her ambiguity. Even in the presence of the strongest faith, the recognition of the ambiguous nature of discernment creates deep humility.

Does this awareness immobilize us? Is the ambiguity so great as to make confident assertions and actions untenable? Not at all. Although discernment is not perfect, even as the star and the circle are not completely congruent, it does have enough overlap with the will of God to create wholeness, offer meaning, generate a sense of rightness, and inspire courage. This degree of fulfillment, even in the face of ambiguity, inspires sufficient confidence for us to perceive the will of God and to regulate our lives by it.

Two other benefits accrue to us through this ambiguity. The partial realization of the will of God in our lives opens the door to doubt. Let us say that you have been invited to give a series of lectures. You prepare as fully as you can, but when the lectures have been written new ideas occur to you. These notions raise questions about the adequacy of the original text of the lectures. The imperfection of the original creation opened the door to doubt, and doubt provided a dynamic that inspired further research and writing. Such is the nature of all our concrete embodiments of the will of God. They all are incomplete; they both reveal and conceal God's purpose. And the ever-present doubt continues to inspire our quest for the perfect will of God.

In addition to the ambiguity and doubt on the human side, we encounter in God the divine mystery. When we approach God, we encounter a certain "thereness" in the will of God. What more can we say about this will that is other than our own? It meets us from beyond; it grasps us with power; it inspires in us a sense of "oughtness." We discern the divine will and act on it. But there is more.

Beyond this divinely revealed will lies mystery. On this "back side of God," as Luther described it, we encounter a dimension of the divine that refuses all efforts of the imagination. The naked encounter with the depth of mystery staggers the imagination and leaves the soul captured by awe. Perhaps in the encounter with mystery nothing else is needed: God and us in inexplicable wonder.

Do we not, therefore, see both the possibility and the threat of the creative imagination in the tasks of discernment?

Seven

Discernment Through Memory

Did you ever have a truth dream, a dream that spoke to you about the deepest part of your life? Sometime ago I read a sermon written by Frederick Buechner, a talented and stimulating writer. He introduced the sermon by relating a dream he had experienced. He called it a truth dream, one from which he awoke with conviction.

In the dream he went to a hotel where he enjoyed a pleasant room. Later he returned to the same hotel, hoping to stay in the same room.

When, in his dream, he was given another room he complained to the desk clerk. The clerk knew exactly which room he meant and so instructed him to always ask for it by name.

"The name of the room was," he said, "Remember."9

If we are to discern the will of God in the present, we must examine its manifestations in our past. The only way to conduct such an investigation is through our memory, the resurrection of the past through our power to recall. We must visit the room called Remember.

Just as the clerk told the dreamer the name of the room, I want to describe to you this room called Remember and tell you how you can enter and listen to its instruction. This room,

96

different from intuition, remains in a fixed place, and you can go there and absorb its meaning again and again.

The way into the future lies in the past, in our memories. And if the way into the future rests in our histories, an acquaintance with them provides the substance of which the future will be made. As the dream suggests, we can enter into the room called Remember, recall eras past, discern their themes, and receive intimations of the future.

In our personal histories we have stored our knowledge of God's will: all that we have been able to discern through a study of scripture, the accumulated wisdom gained through experience, and a narrative of our life journey, the story of meaning that we have been constructing through our interpretations of the occurrences of our lives. These three aspects of our histories contain rudimentary expressions of God's will in our lives. The narrative of our lives fuses together our perception of the will of God revealed in scripture and our accumulated wisdom. If we can find a way to open up this narrative, will it not show us themes, trends, or hints of the future? A friend of mine once summarized it graphically: "The fruit of the future grows from the seed of the past."

In your search for the will of God in the present, it is my intention to point you toward your past, give you reasons why it is important for your future, and point out ways that you can listen to the past as it speaks of your future. In the imagery of Buechner's dream, I want to show you a hallway that leads to the room called Remember, and place your hand on the latch that opens the door to the treasures it holds.

You may have wondered how an excursion into the past can forecast the future. This expectation finds its initial grounding in the creation; God has made us in the divine image for a purpose. Is not each of our lives a concrete expression of one of the purposes of God? Would we have come into being if God had not willed it? Would we continue in life for one moment if God did not will it now? Could we be so narrow as to claim that our naked being alone, being without experience or history, exhausts the intention of God? If God wills our being and sustains our being in this life, certainly the things that happen to us and how we respond to those events compose part of the will of God for us. Thus the narrative we have constructed contains the interpretation of the meaning of our lives. Surely God wills us humans to be, to live, and to seek and find meaning by actualizing the divine intention in our personal histories.

I do not mean that every person's life has been a clear expression of the pure intention of God. The facts quickly repudiate such a preposterous claim. But neither can we make an absolute claim in the opposite direction, that it is possible to live a life that exemplifies nothing of the will of God. No, the will of God, in either a rudimentary or a highly expressive form, exists in us; it is present now in our lives, in every one of us.

If the rudiments of God's will exist in us all, why do we see so many destructive lives? Perhaps for many, even most, the will of God remains an unconscious aspect of their being. It appears occasionally in disguise in consciousness; it comes as a pang of conscience, or as a sense of duty, or even as an urge toward compassion. Possibly these manifestations of God's intention preserve people and society from a worse fate than the current one.

When we single out others as being unconscious of God's will, must we not quickly acknowledge that we also live much of our lives in unawareness? How many days have we lived without a sensitivity to God? Not only people who are spiritually dead but also we who believe share much of the same fate of unconscious living. Does not this fact emphasize the necessity of returning to the room called Remember, the room that enables us to sense what God has been saying in our histories?

Although the will of God always exists in the unconscious, sometimes it presents itself to human consciousness with clarity and is ignored. A directive comes in the form of a sermon, an insight is gained through an intuition, or the witness of a friend suggests a new direction for us. Promptly we turn our attention toward other matters. Even those who believe find ways to look the other way. Does this not suggest another reason why we should intentionally visit the room called Remember?

Among faithful believers, the most common cause of the distortion of God's will occurs because we forget. Far too many Christians suffer from amnesia, the loss of memory. We forget what God has said, we forget who we are, we forget the wisdom of our experience, and in our forgetfulness we lapse into unawareness of God. In that special room we make time to remember. The scriptures often repeatedly enjoin us: "Remember!"

A yet worse form of defacing the intention of God stems from a perverse will, a firm choice for our own will instead of the will of God. Unfortunately we are fallen persons, sinners, who habitually turn away from God in self-assertion and rebellion. Indeed, this turning away blocks, or mars, God's intention. But even human perverseness does not wipe out all the evidence of God's purpose for us.

I am emphasizing the reality of the will of God in our lives, in our personal histories. But I am accounting for the lack of performance of the will of God by noting its unconscious presence and our ignoring, forgetting, and rebelling against it. I hope that you can see the accessibility of the divine intention in your history and at the same time face up to the various ways you have consciously failed to embrace it. Perhaps a look at the way our personal histories are put together will enable us to know our way around the room called Remember.

If we grant that our very being contains one expression of the will of God, how do our personal histories provide data for discerning God's will? In answering this query we must begin with our natures. Already we have focused on the urge toward meaning as central to our being; we have further identified this drive as a disguised search for the will of God; and we have asserted the human impossibility of finding this divine will, which only comes to us as a gift through revelation. But our answers must go beyond this framework. Within this perspective each person brings energy, needs, gifts, potentiality, and vision, all of which participate in the making of meaning.

I have discussed in another place (*To Will God's Will,* pp. 21–33) the way in which we construct meaning in our lives. Five components—events, perceptions, interpretations, connections, and narrative—define the process of making sense of our lives. Each of us engages in this task. As persons of faith, we perceive, interpret, and connect our lives in an awareness of Christ, a process that creates a Christian life-style and witness. We have a Christian understanding of life according to the degree of our faith.

The narrative we create incarnates facets of the divine intention. By recalling that narrative, by revisiting seminal parts of our own story, we can pull back the covering of the intention of God working itself out in our lives. If we can lay bare that structure in one context, the insights will give us a sharper perception of the divine intention in another.

With regard to our histories, centers of meaning create the context for discernment; these centers of meaning are connected by themes and move toward a plot. The drive toward meaning does not move upward and onward like an escalator, nor is it always a face-to-face awareness of the presence of God. Rather, we progress in jumps and spurts through centers of meaning. These centers of meaning appear as a constellation of human hunger and stirring that fuses with the divine intention through a series of events over a limited period of time.

Perhaps these segments of history are best described as eras, a period of time united by a dominant theme. Each era has its own events, its interpretations, and its central meaning. During an era the will of God finds concrete expression in our lives (or sometimes ignorance and abuse of the divine will); we can enter these eras through memory and attempt consciously to discern themes and trends that portend future enfleshments of the will of God. To discern the will of God through these events requires an examination of the content of these eras.

Each era of our lives has a before and an after. Two pathways run from these centers: one comes from behind, drawing into that center meanings from previous eras; the other flows outward into the future, taking the meanings from this era into the next constellation. As we grow older and find deeper meanings, these constellations grow richer and more complex.

The pathway that runs through the centers of meaning connects them, providing a feeling of continuity. Although this continuity may be disrupted, it still offers a more or less unified perspective. In the normal flow of one's life, these pathways have trends and themes that point toward the future; they contain hints, forms, and intimations of the direction of our lives.

The plot of an individual life, like the plot of a movie, suggests its final unveiling. Plot, another word for destiny, describes the ultimate meaning of our lives, that reason for which we were created.

Given this vision of the meaning and the ambiguous but concrete realization of the divine will in human history, can we not at least speculate that these centers have a predictive quality? Thus, to help us in this task of discernment, we must examine the contents of these centers, absorb the energy in them, open ourselves to the intuitions that they inspire, and imaginatively project these themes into the future. For our purposes of discernment, understanding the centers of meaning is critical.

In our discussion of the meaning of meaning, we saw that to have meaning is to have an aim, to be related to a before and after, to express a new creation through the utilization of gifts, to receive recognition and approval from significant persons or groups, or to feel that our being is making a contribution to something beyond ourselves. Even as we recall this description, the inadequacy of the definition cannot be concealed. Confessing that the effort is not complete, these phrases at least provide a beginning point to explore the centers of meaning in our lives and their predictive quality.

By a center of meaning I am identifying a period of time, long or short, when we experienced a feeling of significance, a unity with God, the expression of God's will. This significance may have come from the affirmation of others or from a deep sense of satisfaction in ourselves. This center had specific content, like place and activity, but it had more than that; it had a certain ambience, a feeling that cannot be reduced to the component elements. These centers of meaning are often revelations of the meaning of our lives, not a whole life but aspects of it. Certainly there are seemingly meaningful experiences that are as sinful as the devil himself, but I'm not talking about these perverse excursions in pseudo-meaning. I am

thinking of the person with a heart for God who in certain
moments finds deep satisfaction, even awareness, in doing
what pleases God. These are the kinds of experiences that have
revelatory possibilities.

Perhaps a description of some of the elements in these
centers will provide clues for recognition. A center of meaning
has a geographical setting—where we were when the meaning
occurred in our lives. It also has time limits—we can usually
say, "It began when . . . and seemed to last until . . ." Although
these boundaries are soft, they carve out eras that can be
thought of as a whole. I think of these elements as constituting
a revelatory era.

Into these periods marked off by a beginning and an end
come people who play a prominent role in the drama of our
lives. We can name them; their faces shine before us; the memory of them brings joy and delight, or sometimes sorrow, to our
lives. The situation and the people in it call forth responses
within us. Sometimes we are called to use our gifts in new
creations—art, music, culture, or service. Mixed with the influence of others and free choice, the hand of providence also
can be traced. We often feel a force or energy outside ourselves
operative in the events of our lives. These concurrences also
had an emotional dimension—some inspired joy and excitement; sometimes these events brought pain and the experience
of a loss of meaning and sadness. When an era ends we are
often left with a sense of wholeness or completion. Perhaps
some happening brings a sense of closure to a chapter of our
lives, and although the meaning does not erode, we know it no
longer holds our reason for being. With the closure, a particular era of our lives has ended. In the ending, the beginnings of
a new era can already be discerned.

You have probably felt throughout this abstract description a certain lostness. To make my meaning more specific I
will illustrate the construction of a center of meaning in my life.
As well as school, marriage, children, and creative ministries,
the Lay Witness Mission era of my life offers a clear example
of a center of meaning.

The Lay Witness Mission originated in Phenix City, Alabama, but the setting later included Atlanta, Georgia, and extended from there nationwide. The era began in 1961 and lasted for me, in some measure, until 1971. In this decade a number of significant people came into my life to shape me and the ministry, among them Chuck Carpenter, Thomas A. Carruth, Milford Chewning, G. Ross Freeman, Andrew Gallman, A. Taplin Hanson, Jerry Powell, James Sells, and John Taylor. Each seemed to fulfill a special role: model, encourager, instructor, mentor, companion, fellow worker. The circumstances of my life in the church during those years, aided by such people with their gifts, combined to bring forth the vision of renewing Christ's church. With that vision of vital, witnessing lay men and women, open doors appeared for me to lead renewal weekends. As a result of these came affirmations from participants, church leaders, and my own spirit. These providential signs inspired courage to proceed with greater challenges and risks. My own responses were a mixture of peace, joy, excitement, and fulfillment. The Lay Witness Mission era, for me, lasted about ten years, marked by the first one in 1961 and the ten-year celebration in 1971. Even though, twenty-five to thirty years later, missions still occur, their meaning for me peaked after five or six years and tailed during the next four or five. The celebration at the end of the first decade marked the fulfillment of that center and the launching of a new, though undefined, era in my life and ministry.

Both at the time and in the two decades since, the conviction of being in and doing the will of God was present. This does not mean that in everything I was doing the will of God. Problems, frustrations, and sinfulness impeded God's purposes. Yet I find myself possessed with a conviction that the divine intention prevailed in my personal history.

This center of meaning contained both fulfillment and a forecast—the dual paths. The path leading into this center had flowed from previous centers that could be elaborated in fuller ways, showing how the content of previous meaning centers prepared me for this one. For example, the Lay Witness Mission became my boldest experiment in ministry up to that point. But I had, from the beginning, been an experimenter.

Evidence for this assessment can be seen in my having begun
a radio program during my senior year in high school and in
my Saturday-night youth rally for the community of my first
pastorate. This recognition illustrates that vital elements in the
Lay Witness Mission era can be traced to earlier, predictive
experiences.

But this center contained not only elements from the past
but also seed of the future. Two illustrations will be sufficient
to clarify how this era was predictive of my future. The Lay
Witness Mission era revealed to me that I was a religious
entrepreneur, a dreamer, an initiator, a risk-taker. Whatever
ingredients combine to form an entrepreneur—gifts, preferences, tastes, perceptual systems, drives—this characterizes me
as much as my hands or my heart. Knowing this, I should
expect the future to be met and shaped by this way of seeing
reality and this way of being in the world and doing whatever
I do in ministry.

As a matter of fact, this gift (sometimes it seems like a
curse) has remained a driving force in my life for nearly thirty
years. At age fifty-five, when I set aside a few weeks to contemplate the remainder of my life, the central theme remained—
innovation in the ministry of Christ. The crucial question that
emerged is, Is it the will of God for me to be a religious
entrepreneur, or is my life a mistake controlled by a sick, blind
ego? I suspect a vote taken of my public would be split. But in
spite of sin, blindness, and the perversions evident in me, I
have an even deeper conviction that this is who I am and this
is what I am to do to glorify God. What more can one do than
be faithful to the highest he or she knows?

Another aspect of the Lay Witness Mission era also has
been predictive. In the predawn hours of this ministry I wrote
my first book. The writing itself occurred in a strange way. I
became obsessed with the idea of writing a book on prayer. I
could not get it out of my mind. Finally, one evening after
going to bed I found that I could not sleep, so I got up, went
to the church, and spent all night writing my ideas on a yellow
pad. When I finished the first draft, a sense of relief swept over
me, a feeling I was to experience numerous times in the future.

I typed and mimeographed the manuscript, one hundred copies at a time. I made them available to classes, to members of the church, and to people who attended schools I conducted. All these initiatives were predictive of my publishing efforts in the next twenty years.

Although I wrote books, articles, and pamphlets by the score during the next twenty years, I never thought of myself as a writer, even though I had manuscripts accepted by five publishers. My identity as a writer remained hidden to me. Then one day a strange thing happened. My editor, who had been working with me for twelve years, noted a statement I made about being a writer. She said, "That's the first time in all these years I've ever heard you refer to yourself as a writer."

That encounter marked a transition in my identity and sense of call. Later on I discovered that this call as a writer remained with me. A decade later, as I spent those quiet hours of meditation in the desert, when I projected activities for the remainder of my life, I found it impossible to think of myself as not writing. Perhaps this struggle suggests a sickness, such as a compulsion or an obsession, rather than a revelation of God's will. Whatever, the conviction remains and I imagine you can guess my suspicion that both the desire and the energy to write come from God.

In this piece of narrative you can see the setting for the Lay Witness Mission era; the people who at different times came into my life to correct or affirm the ministry; my own responses of fulfillment and assurance; the emotional dimensions of anxiety and risk mixed with joy and fulfillment; the confidence that "something" outside myself was directing the events of my life; the sense of fullness and wholeness at the end of the era. I hope this slice of biography has made clear what I mean by a center of meaning and has also shown how one's gifts and preferences become evident through creative engagement. The gifts and possibilities drawn out by the providences of our lives give us a clue, at least, about our destiny. The plot—that is, the future actualization of my gifts through intuition and creative imagination—will probably be that of a religious or Christian entrepreneur. At least all my visions of the future include creation, risk, change—the fruition of beginnings in an earlier era of my life. How could a future be different if we are called to actualize our created potential?

One possible misunderstanding needs safeguarding. The description of my gifts and sense of call does not provide content for others to imitate. The personal illustrations suggest that all of us can identify the gifts and call of God in our centers of meaning and use that discernment to help clarify directions for the future. Furthermore, because my vocation has been that of a minister, the illustration has church and religious content; the meaning center of non-clerics may be found in secular structures. Surely we know by now that the will of God cannot be confined to religious settings.

Memory and Discernment

After this description of the predictive element in our centers of meaning, consider again the central question we are seeking to answer. How can we discern the will of God for the future through events of the past? How can we look back to see ahead? The following process of discovery will help you answer this question.

The first step requires that we begin with the centers of meaning in our lives. Identify those centers that hold the meaning of your life. Each of these probably holds common themes, or threads of meaning. To ferret out these threads, answer these questions regarding each center.

1. When did this era begin?
2. What was the setting geographically? In the larger society?
3. Who were the significant persons?
4. What gifts did the setting evoke? What potential did it actualize?
5. What feelings—emotional responses—most often accompanied the occurrences?
6. How was God at work in these persons and events? What especially did God seem to be doing through you?
7. What were the dominant threads, or trends, in the center? What are their roots in the past? Their possible expressions in the future?

8. What are your feelings about the closing of the era? Muse over these insights and pay attention to the intuitions they inspire for the future.

To work productively with these data, begin with the current era of your life. Answer all the questions except the one about the ending of the era. This will place you squarely in the present. From this perspective you can explore previous centers of meaning. Having the data of the present in your mind like a filter will sift out the elements in your past that speak to the present.

When you have completed the reflection on your centers of meaning, ask your deeper self for a symbol of your life. I suspect that the symbol will manifest itself in all the centers of meaning, and it too is predictive for your future. I have always been attracted to the image of an explorer.

All these data, approached in faith, will enable you to grasp more deeply God's intention for you in the larger scheme of salvation. Suppose that you have engaged in an intensive review of our centers of meaning; you have identified a number of themes in your life that occur with a degree of regularity. You stand in the present with the urgent question: What does God want me to do with my life? You are created in God's image with a hunger for God's will, you have chosen a symbol as expressive of your life, you are free to choose your course, and you have discerned the movement of God in your history through your centers of meaning; these actions of God within your history give you a convictional base about God and the ways of God, and out of that conviction you have energy that gives you courage to act.

I began with a reference to a room called Remember. In this discussion I have invited you into the room to explore the furnishings and to feel the ambience of those centers of meaning in your one and only life.

Eight

Doing the Will of God

For several years I have been nourished by the writings of Carlo Carretto, a mystic, saint, and visionary. In his book *The God Who Comes* he gives a description of "newness" that is, for me, a motivator to action.

If you ask me how God has revealed himself to me I should reply, "He reveals himself as newness."

I am not newness, I am old age. Everything in me is old, boring, repetitive.

But when I search God's face I find newness.

God never repeats himself.

When I pray I search for this newness of God. When I contemplate I hope for his newness.

And it is the only thing that never bores me.

That is why I understand that if I do not pray I am up against the wall of my "old age"; if I do not contemplate I am without "prophecy," if I don't nurse at the breast of divine life, grace is lost to me.

And who am I without the newness of God?

Who am I without prophecy?

What use am I without grace?[10]

108

To discern the will of God and to enact it brings new-ness—in one's personal life, in history, in the world. Is there vision greater than the one that sees our concrete responses of obedience to God as the creation of newness?

What is the meaning of discernment if not to do the will of God, if not to participate in the creation of newness? If we listed all the negative purposes of discernment, perhaps at the head of the list would be "speculation." The discernment of the divine intention can never be for the purpose of detached reflection. Discernment requires action. In our obedience the will of God is done on earth; God purposes to be incarnate in human history; the person who obeys finds fulfillment and meaning.

From one perspective, all that has been written thus far points to the free and eager enactment of God's will in our lives. If doing the will of God is our supreme good, its perform-ance yields good temporally and eternally. If humans hunger for the divine will, only doing it brings satisfaction. If the inten-tion of God has been written in the human psyche, fulfillment of the potential depends on concrete actualizations. If the psy-che flashes intuitions of God's will into consciousness, and the creative imagination forms these vague images, they do so only to flesh out these new forms. And we look back in our lives not merely to get hints about the future but also to embrace it as our participation in the purpose of God.

To stop with images in the mind obstructs the central intention of God—incarnation, to express the divine will con-cretely in people and in history. Without action, discernment becomes the most gross perversion of Christian faith—Gnosti-cism. According to the Gnostics, one only had to have knowl-edge *(gnosis)*. With respect to discernment, the Gnostic contented himself or herself with personal enlightenment of the divine will. Without genuine obedience to the divine wis-dom, the eager seeker slides into the slimy pit of Gnostic specu-lation. So the task before us focuses on free obedience that fleshes out the will of God in concrete choices and actions.

This obedience to God's will produces yet another mode of discernment. *We know the will of God by doing the will of God—*

those words might be inscribed on the banner of our lives. Thus our effort in discernment has a twin focus: the discernment of God's will so that we may enact it and the discernment of our actions so that we may see in them the will of God made visible through us.

Our discussion of the will of God in the foundation of human existence suggests that "to be" is automatically "to be in relation to God's purpose." If indeed the will of God has been written into the structure of our being as a ground plan, and if certain gifts and preferences have a genetic reference, the will of God is not alien to our deepest nature. We are estranged from it; our self-centeredness blinds us and diverts us. Still, something within us hungers for the voice of the Other that tells us the choices to make or the path to follow. This hunger, redeemed by Christ and restored by his salvation, has a refinement that awakens a desire for God's will. A word of caution: We must never accept uncritically our desires as expressive of the divine will, but to condemn all human desire as a manifestation of sin errs on the other side.

If the divine will has been written within us, creation has also given us certain capacities to translate divine intention and human hunger into specific, concrete behavior. The intuition constantly flashes images of the divine will into human consciousness. Whether this faculty of knowing, apart from the usual rational process, arises from creation or involves at times the free movement of the Holy Spirit I cannot say, but the intuition at times gives us intimations of God's intention.

Both the internal impulse of intuition and the external data of events are resources for the imagination. Intuition functions within our depths, and events come about through persons and experiences; these provide data to the creative imagination. We have seen how the events of our lives cluster in centers of meaning; reflection on these centers also feeds the creative imagination. The imagination receives substance from the content of scripture and, in particular, the events in Jesus' life. Brooding over this material, the creative imagination pictures concrete embodiments of God's will and the possible choices and actions in one's life. Between the image of the divine will and actually doing it stands a person's will. But we must do God's will if we are to know God's will. Because none of our actions perfectly demonstrate God's will and all our choices result in a dialectical situation of yes and no, how can we have a degree of assurance that we have done the will of God in our lives?

To answer this crucial question, we return to our root metaphor, Christ, the embodiment of the will of God. If we view him as "the will of God made flesh," whatever testified to his being the Son of God provides a model for our discernment of God's will made flesh in us. In the fifth chapter of the Fourth Gospel, Jesus encountered some Jewish critics. They questioned his integrity and his being God's Son—that is, his being the incarnation of God's will. Critics will always ask, "How can you claim to do the will of God?" The way Christ handled the critics' doubts is instructive. The need for confirmation arises from both our own doubts and, at times, the doubts of others. Jesus' responses reveal the sources of assurance for our choices.

Jesus disclaimed his own authority. He made it clear to his accusers that he did not manifest the will of God apart from God's action in him. His discernment came to him from God, and he spoke what was given. Jesus claimed that God acted on his consciousness, perhaps with intuition and images, to reveal the divine will. He did not think of these revelations as originating from his own genius but from God. The attitude of Jesus instructs us ordinary humans, with all our capacities for novelty and creativity, that we depend ultimately on God to speak through these capacities and guide us to do God's will.

Jesus also claimed that his discernment was correct when he said, "I seek not my own will but the will of him who sent me" (John 5:30). Jesus actualized God's will because his own will did not get in the way. None of us can do God's will until we surrender our own will to God's or, stated positively, until we will God's will. Jesus had made this choice. Later he would teach his followers to pray, "Thy will be done"; in the last hours he would demonstrate the integrity of his profession to the Jews and his instruction to the disciples when through sweat, blood, and struggle he prayed, "Not my will but thine be done." In these instances Christ showed us that, to do God's will, we must choose God's will over our own.

Lest we miss his testimony, Jesus further emphasized this prerequisite. "If anyone's will is to do God's will, he or she shall know whether the teaching is from God or whether I am speaking on my own authority" (John 7:17, alt.). If persons want to know whether their actions conform to God's will, they must first desire God's will—will the will of God for their lives. And Jesus indicated that if they do so, God's intention will become evident to them. This indication further underscores the impossibility of discovering the will of God as a detached observer.

Now we have two elements in doing the will of God— surrendering our wills to God and listening to God's speech from beyond us, a speech heard in the voices of persons, the convergence of events, and the providential acts of God. The element of listening raises still another crucial question: How can we distinguish between God's voice and our own? Possibly no question drives to the heart of discernment more than this one. The answer lies in two directions: internal evidences of the call of God and external means of confirming it.

In this encounter Jesus said, "As I hear, I judge [discern]" (John 5:30). This statement suggests that God speaks, and what God says provides discernment. Any effort to describe the tones of God's speech will always be partial and open to reevaluation. The free God may speak in whatever ways God wills. Having made this confession, we may say that both personal experience and the tradition carried in the Christian community offer wisdom at this point.

In the first place, God speaks with gentleness. The divine voice usually does not come with condemnation or harshness. An old monk once said, "Jesus speaks with a tiny voice." Gentle, not harsh; soft, not loud. In a setting that could have evoked both harshness and loudness, because the disciples had denied and forsaken him, Jesus addressed them very simply: "Children, have you any fish?"

Perhaps persistence describes the second most characteristic quality of the voice of God. God does not speak once and retreat into silence. In the scripture, God asks, "How often? How long? How many times must I speak to you?" Israel must indeed be a paradigm of the persistence of God. In Jeremiah the Lord says, "I have seen your abominations, your adulteries and neighings, your lewd harlotries, on the hills in the field. Woe to you, O Jerusalem! *How long will it be before you are made clean?*" (13:27, emphasis added). When God calls to a particular vocation or guides us to a certain life-style, we often discern the call by the persistence of God's speaking. Even when human beings are dull of hearing and resist the divine will, these inadequacies do not deter the graciousness and persistence of God.

God also speaks with clarity. When confusion reigns in a particular judgment, wisdom demands that we wait until the static clears. Paul made the principle clear to the Corinthians: "God is not a God of confusion but of peace" (1 Cor. 14:33).

The biblical record suggests that God speaks specifically to persons. To the disciples Jesus said, "Go into all the world" (see Matt. 28:19–20). The commission to evangelize came in clear, specific guidance again to Paul and Barnabas: "Set apart for me Barnabas and Saul for the work to which I have called them" (Acts 13:2). One word of caution must be heeded. The word of God may come to us with clarity, and the confusion in our hearts may result from our subtle resistance to God's will.

God's speech also has a convictional character. When God speaks, that word grasps us with an inexplicable certainty; sometimes it has a compelling urgency that demands immediate choice. The conviction generates the courage to choose and act. The experience of hearing God empowers the action God wills. Did not the paralyzed man who was carried on a stretcher to Jesus' house experience this convincing, empowering speech? "Get up. Take up your mat and go home." Thus the convictional empowering aspect of God's speech offers another way of discernment.

In the long tradition of discernment, the people of God have always depended on the restful state of soul as a clue to the divine will. When God speaks, the divine will issues in peace. Both peace and clarity indicate the absence of confusion. Clarity suggests the absence of rational confusion; peace, the absence of emotional confusion. But peace also has the positive quality of soothing and strengthening the soul. Whereas clarity of intention speaks to direction, peace speaks to the "ought" or duty; it lays to rest the moral imperative within.

A further word regarding these characteristics of God's speech must be heeded. Each characteristic of the speech of God can be distorted and perverted by our own desires or the peculiar circumstance of our hearing. The capacity of humans for self-deception seems limitless. Constant vigilance must keep our memory fresh that we are dealing with the great God who cannot finally be defined by our categories. Dogmatism regarding subjective experience must be resisted. But this warning does not mean that we should ignore our subjective experience. Could we if we tried? Although we have examined the biblical and traditional wisdom regarding the speech of God, what we experience in the soul must correlate with certain other external factors. This brings us to the external ways of God's speech.

The text to which we have appealed—"If I bear witness to myself, my testimony is not true; there is another who bears witness to me, and I know that the testimony which he bears to me is true" (John 5:31–32)—provides a transition from the subjective to the objective. Is not Jesus in this confession stating the warning in another way? If people testify that God has spoken, that they have been led by God, or that the will of God is this or that, does not their witness demand authentication from other sources to protect them from self-delusion? Jesus' point seems to be, If I am the only one who agrees with my discernment, and if no other authority confirms it, my guidance may be open to serious question. To what did Jesus appeal as authoritative? His sources of confirmation provide a model for us in discerning the voice of God from our own internal longings. Proper distinction saves us from self-deception and illusion.

First, Jesus claimed the witness of his forerunner as confirmation of his action. John the Baptist gave this testimony: "Behold, the Lamb of God, who takes away the sin of the world!" (John 1:29). Jesus recalled further legitimizing testimony. "And John bore witness, 'I saw the Spirit descend as a dove from heaven, and it remained on him. I myself did not know him; but he who sent me to baptize with water said to me, "He on whom you see the Spirit descend and remain, this is he who baptizes with the Holy Spirit." And I have seen and have borne witness that this is the Son of God' " (John 1:32–34).

Who are the John the Baptists in our lives? Are they not our brothers and sisters in the Christian community? In our efforts to do God's will, they listen to our claim; they look at our actions to help us see the will of God. The responses of the community of faith either confirm our discernment or call it into question. Therefore, we should heed what God says through the lips of fellow believers.

Perhaps this suggests that we should not leave to chance the reactions of fellow believers but, rather, inquire directly of them concerning our decisions. Should we not select a mature member of the community before whom we can lay open our life and from whom we can seek wisdom? Yet this act offers only one of dozens of ways that God addresses us through the faithful members of the Christian community; consider friendship, or the chance response of an acquaintance, or a sermon scripture, or a hymn.

In the second place Jesus said, "These very works which I am doing, bear me witness that the Father has sent me" (John 5:36). Jesus indicated that his actions demonstrated the authenticity and validity of his person—deeds validated his personhood. Note that he said they "bear me witness." His own behavior revealed to him God's will. Because his actions were public, others too, by looking, could discern the presence of God in them.

Behavior authenticates the will of God. Do not our actions reveal the intention of God? In this instance the serious seeker for God's will depends not on subjective feelings for discernment but on specific actions. These actions have an objective quality open to all who care to inspect them. So behavior validates discernment and stands outside our subjective feelings, open for all to see.

In addition to his works, Jesus experienced confirmation by the voice of God. He was probably recalling the voice at the baptism or on the Mount of Transfiguration; the voice from heaven comes only in special situations, certainly not our common experience. Only once have I heard someone make a serious claim to this experience. He was Jewish. A Christian witness had influenced him. In the struggle to determine if Jesus were Messiah, he cried out to God, "Is Jesus your Messiah?"

A voice came back, "He is the Messiah."

Although some may wish for such a direct communication, and others hope that it never happens to them, history suggests that the "voice from heaven" is not the usual way of God. How, then, are we to understand this external authority that speaks to us?

If we return to the revelation of God in Christ as our norm, perhaps we will discern that since Jesus Christ incarnates the will of God, he is the voice of God. In him God spoke to us and made the eternal word accessible to us. In the gospel texts we possess a record of the life and sayings of this "God with us." Because we believe that these assertions are dependable, we can listen to the word God has spoken and does speak through the person of Jesus. Jesus Christ is the Word of God outside us, coming to us, addressing us.

When our activities express the spirit or the aim of Christ, he confirms us. He assures us that our choices are of God. If we do what Jesus did, in the spirit with which he did it, he grants an assurance that our choices are the will of God. By the same criterion those actions that belie or contradict the Spirit of Christ also evidence unfaithfulness to the will of God. So, in Christ, we have a norm by which to discern whether our actions express or break God's will.

In addition to these external norms, Jesus appealed to one other source of external authority, the scriptures. To the critical Jews he said, "You search the scriptures . . . and it is they that bear witness to me" (John 5:39). When we appeal to

Christ's model of discerning the will of God, this statement signifies that sacred scripture, in its entirety, bears witness to Christ. You could object that this reasoning is both circular and redundant. We appeal to scripture that witnesses to Christ whom we have claimed to be the will of God. Although these charges have a degree of truth, they do not obviate the appeal to the long tradition in scripture. The tradition—the broad sense conveyed in scripture—comes to focus in Christ, but the numerous insights, illustrations, and instructions in the text enable us to understand Christ more fully as God's will. In shorthand, the scriptures bear witness to Christ and Christ appeals to the scriptures. The river that flows down the mountain contains the same water as the reservoir into which it flows. But the form of the water in the reservoir is different.

This principle, therefore, invites a review of the whole of scripture as a revelation of God's will. In many forms through the years, the scriptures describe which behavior conforms to the will of God and which incurs judgment. This larger mirror provides us with varied reflections of the divine intention, reflections that enable us to discern the will of God in our actions. Keep in mind that we are seeking discernment to act, and we are examining our acts to be assured that we are doing the will of God.

Thus far we have indicated that our efforts to discern God's will are to do God's will. The choice to do God's will has elements of ambiguity, and we have set forth a tradition of wisdom—both the internal and the external kinds—to help us act with confidence. This appeal lays out both the private and the public aspect of discerning the will of God.

Several important issues in this discussion beg for attention—the issues of obedience and personal integrity, irregular grace, and appropriate humility. Look at the first issue. Does not the surrender of the self violate the integrity of one's personhood? Did not God create us unique selves with the intention that we should actualize that self? And does not the abdication of our own will to an alien will render that intention void?

Our response to this question should begin with an examination of "alien." Is God's will alien to us, and does it invalidate human freedom? We have presupposed that we human beings were created by God and for God. We have indicated that God's intention has been written into the structure of our being and that to do God's will results in our highest good and deepest fulfillment. In our discussion of the manner in which God generally approaches us, human freedom and personhood are kept intact. Thus to do God's will does not violate personhood; it fulfills it. And, to the contrary, to deny God's will actually distorts personhood and ultimately destroys it. True freedom is to will to do what God intends. Perhaps an equally important question might be whether we can have true personhood apart from surrender to the will of God.

The second issue stems from the knowledge that we do the will of God by obeying the commandments. To say it another way, "When our actions violate the teaching of scripture or the sayings of Christ, can these actions ever be the will of God?" At first glance we would say no, but look further.

In a seminar I conducted, an Episcopal priest gave me a term for this contradictory behavior. He called it "irregular grace," or "strange providence." This providence, or grace, appears most often when an action in a particularly ambiguous situation violates the law of God but fulfills the love revealed in Jesus. For example, God commanded us, "Remember the sabbath day, to keep it holy" (Ex. 20:8). But Jesus, without hesitation, healed on the Sabbath and plucked grain for food on the Sabbath. When questioned, he answered, "Man was not made for the sabbath, but the sabbath for man" (see Mark 2:23–28). He articulates the principle that when a commandment violates the law of love, love prevails over the commandment.

This principle has relevance to several thorny issues: divorce, abortion, homosexuality, and sexual intercourse outside marriage. Take divorce as an example. Is divorce always wrong? Can it ever be the will of God? The intention of God for the family has been made clear. "Therefore a man leaves his father and his mother and cleaves to his wife, and they become one flesh" (Gen. 2:24). This intention of God was reiterated by Christ. " 'For this reason a man shall leave his father and mother and be joined to his wife, and the two shall become one flesh.' . . . What therefore God has joined together, let not man put asunder" (Mark 10:7–9).

God's commandment regarding marriage is clear. Is there ever a circumstance in which the love of God contradicts the commandment of God? There are instances in which two persons who are married to each other cannot put their lives together productively, to say nothing of peaceably. Their relationship becomes increasingly destructive, and their conflict has painful consequences for their children. Is it the will of God that they fulfill a legal or moral contract at the cost of health, happiness, and productive living, both their own and their children's? Some would testify that the will of God in this instance can be served by divorce. If so, this is what my priest friend meant by "irregular grace," a grace given that enables a person to break one commandment in order to keep another.

Look at another example. Does this "strange grace" ever come in the expression of sexual relations outside marriage? At first glance we say no. The commandments are clear: "Thou shalt not commit adultery." Jesus said, "You have heard that it was said, 'You shall not commit adultery.' But I say to you that every one who looks at a woman lustfully has already committed adultery with her in his heart" (Matt. 5:27–28). Paul seems to be explicit that adulterers and fornicators shall have no part in the kingdom of God (1 Cor. 6:9–11).

Granted the clarity of these directives, to which I certainly ascribe, I am still haunted by a line from N. Richard Nash's play *The Rainmaker*. In the play the Rainmaker seduces and has sexual relations with a spinster daughter of the rancher. The woman's brother, enraged, threatens to kill the man. But his father, realizing the transformation that has come to his daughter through the illicit relation, takes the pistol from his son. He then makes a haunting statement: "Noah, you're so full of what's right you can't see what's good."[11]

These references in no way intend to annul the commandments of God. Divorce and adultery are wrong. Yet some of us who were reared in a black-and-white, right-and-wrong, moral-istic form of religion may be blinded to the possibility of God's working even in sins of disobedience. I hope we will not be so obsessed with what is right that we cannot see what is good.

All these instances that bespeak strange providence and irregular grace point to the third issue—an appropriate humility. Only by grace can any of us discern and do the will of God. All our expressions of that will, at best, are ambiguous. No expression is ever perfect. An appropriate humility demands some self-criticism toward our own performance, knowing that our strengths give us no cause to boast, nor do our weaknesses plunge us into despair. And in light of our own imperfections, we must give a place to those whose choices are different from our own and whose lives demonstrate a different form of weakness.

I want to tell you a story, an imaginary story, but not totally imaginary because I have known such people. I have experienced them in different settings. I tell you about them because their experience offers you a chance to struggle with the grace of God and perhaps the judgment of God.

A Story

A certain family had a strange and wonderful thing happen through their two sons. Like any family, the parents wanted the sons to express the family dreams as well as their own uniqueness. Hattie Thompson, the mother, just knew that when she was carrying the younger, there was something different about that boy.

Sure enough, he grew up to have a "mind of his own"; he knew what was expected but had the hardest time doing it. His older brother, Brad, had always been so different. Brad had been a model child. He listened well to his father's teaching and tried to live his life like a Thompson should

Chuck, the younger, was different, a real hell-raiser. He worried his mother and enraged his father. His companions, his life-style, and his aimless life made family relations hard to maintain. He drifted farther and farther from home. Sometimes months passed with no contact.

Brad was just the opposite. He graduated from college, got

a job with the local bank, and married. In all his life-shaping decisions he tried to do what he had been taught. His parents were pleased.

In time Brad had a son of his own. He named his son Sam. He thought his life as happy and full as anyone's could be— happy as could be, that is, until one afternoon Brad came home unexpectedly and found Cindy, his wife, in bed with his best friend. His world shattered; his self-esteem was flatter than a basketball without air. A mixture of rage, fear, guilt, and disappointment filled his soul. He felt paralyzed and helpless. What should he do? Where could God be in this pain?

Brad prayed, really prayed. Although he moved out of the house, he kept in touch with Cindy and Sam. One day it struck him: "Forgive Cindy." She had asked him a dozen times. In some ways Brad blamed himself. He had been absorbed in his work. Perhaps he was to blame for her loneliness and feelings of being abandoned. Had his work become his mistress? One evening when they went out to dinner, he told Cindy that he did forgive her. He asked her forgiveness. Life went on with scars.

Chuck showed up at his father's house about the time Brad and Cindy got back together. Hattie had the whole family over for dinner. After the meal, Chuck disclosed his own deep, dark secret. He stunned the whole family.

"I know you all wonder," he began, "why I stay in San Francisco and never come home. Well, I've decided to tell you the long and painful story. I have a problem, one I've had a long time, and I have always been afraid to tell you for fear that you would be humiliated and reject me.

"Since I was in my late teens I've had homosexual leanings. I had some experiences before leaving home, but I never liked my life-style, and even when friends told me 'I was just born that way,' my pain never lessened. In Frisco I was far away and thought of you all as little as possible. My anxiety was less that way.

"I had been living with a male lover when, a few months ago, a strange thing happened. One evening I was having a beer at the Blue Bell Bar down the street from my apartment. A beautiful, shapely young woman across the bar caught my eye. After another beer and several exchanges of glances she came over and sat down next to me. She was delightful, so different from Anna, who turned down my invitation to the junior prom.

Her warmth, her charm, her interest in me awakened feelings in me I didn't know were there.

"Nothing more happened that evening. But Jessica—that's her name—and I began seeing each other. I moved away from my roommate after several bitter arguments and threats. I told Jessica everything about myself. My past seemed not to destroy her interest in me.

"One night Jessica asked me over for dinner. You can imagine the mood—wine, music, candlelight, the whole bit. That evening Jessica made love to me. I didn't know it could happen. It was like a miracle. I felt loved, loved by a woman. It was as though I had walked out of a deep, dark wood—and now I was in the light.

"Jessica and I are planning to be married."

By this time Chuck was on his feet. Chuck's dad slowly rose from the table, walked over, and hugged him. "You are my son. I love you and I want us all—Hattie and me, Brad, Cindy, and Sam, and you and Jessica—to be a family."

And was the will of God done? This story gives flesh-and-blood concreteness to the issues we raised. There was the neglect of the husband, the affair of the wife, the practices of the son that raised some questions for his parents. These violated the will of God, and yet in some strange way God brought good out of evil. In each case love triumphed over law.

Is it possible that we must at times find the will of God mixed up with human frailty and sin, find it in the pain and suffering of souls that have gone astray and cannot find their way back to the path, find it in those unforgivable sins that all of us had rather avoid thinking about?

In our day some people will have to find God's will there because that is where they are. The pathway into the will of God always begins with our next step.

Nine

The Will of God and the Problem of Evil

In our discussion of the will of God, we have affirmed a loving God as manifest in the person of Jesus. In this incarnate form the divine nature has been exposed as gracious, caring, and powerful—powerful enough to raise the dead. We have examined those human capacities for discerning the divine will, including an assurance given in doing the will of God. So long as life flows smoothly, these capacities and processes provide adequate confidence to proceed with our life choices. But when we experience the contradiction of this loving God in life, troublesome questions arise that complicate our functioning. How do we find the will of God when catastrophes disrupt life, when some senseless evil undermines every ounce of meaning that life has held, or when death invades the carefully constructed structures of our lives? To be honest with ourselves we must examine those commonly experienced contradictions in their various aspects and see how they may be resolved.

Life's Catastrophes

Most people have few questions about the divine will when life flows smoothly. For one group it is a matter of indifference, and for another it is a matter of presumption. Maybe for another the wholeness of life evokes a sense of gratitude. But these reactions change when life does not proceed according to expectations.

Disappointments, unfulfilled plans, and catastrophes come in a thousand ways, requiring us to question their perspective. These disruptions come like mighty tides of water that break the dam and flood all the villages below, like explosions that gut buildings and destroy them, like erosions that undermine the foundations of great structures—so great is the power of evil in the destruction of meaning in our lives. In one instance a woman's life shatters because she learns that her "faithful" husband has betrayed her trust. The shock breaks apart her world and leaves her with doubts about her own worth, about her vision of a positive future, and about the love of God for her. This betrayal breaks the dam that holds the pool of meaning for her, and in that moment of awareness the last drop of purpose drains out of her life. How does a person find the will of God when meaning itself has dried up?

In another instance the daughter of devoted parents, their only daughter, is killed in an automobile accident when a drunken driver runs a stop sign and plows into her car. Such a senseless act explodes the meaning in their family and guts their hope, leaving only a hollow shell. How are these parents to discern the will of God in this senseless catastrophe? How will they explain it to themselves so they can go on with their lives?

In a third situation a man invests his life savings in a business venture. Through a combination of adverse economic circumstances and mismanagement, the business fails and he loses every cent, in addition to being saddled with a heavy indebtedness. In just a few years the foundation of his life is eroded by a growing anxiety and eventually the collapse of the business. The unimaginable end finally comes; he files for bankruptcy. This failure leaves him with self-doubt as well as doubts about the goodness and concern of God. Where does he begin to discern God's will?

These instances, to some degree, have a common character—the misuse of human freedom. Although these events are troublesome enough, perhaps more difficult to explain are those instances of natural evil over which humans have no control. An earthquake in Mexico City kills hundreds of innocent victims, and thousands more are left without homes and livelihood. How do we explain this senseless waste in a world created by a loving God? A tidal wave sweeps across an island, wiping out lives, homes, and businesses. Nature becomes angry—so at least it appears—and belches forth anger on helpless, innocent victims. A volcano erupts on Mount St. Helens and pours out molten lava by the ton, searing and consuming all in its path. Could not nature be kinder?

Nature acts as a vicious, even capricious judge through these forces outside our control. But on occasion nature's aberrations come closer. What are we to say to the couple who has longed for a child for several years? Finally the wife becomes pregnant, and during the months of waiting the prospective parents are filled with images of fulfillment and happiness that this new life will bring them. When the child is born he is grossly deformed. Not only is he hideous to view, but he will never have mind enough to care for himself. How can these parents believe in a good God who loves them and wills the highest good for human beings? How is the will of God related to these aberrations in nature?

In other instances nature's deficiency may not be as vicious as an earthquake, but its lack of resilience can be just as painful. Consider the man who enters the hospital for simple surgery on his nose. The test of a small piece of tissue indicates malignancy, and the man learns that he has cancer. The disease cannot be conquered, and in the months that follow it eats away until finally it attacks his brain and the man dies.

Or consider the woman who all her life feared losing her mind. At sixty-two she begins to lose her grip on reality. The stark terror of insanity freezes her tongue so that she cannot discuss either her loss of memory or her fear of the inevitable, even with her family. Her bout with Alzheimer's disease continues for three years until she is institutionalized. Nothing can be done to help her, and eventually she ceaselessly mumbles senseless sounds; her eyes acquire a glaze that seems to shield her from seeing anyone who visits. Does not this deficiency in nature raise questions for us about the nature of ultimate reality, its power and its goodness?

Other examples could be produced, but these describe clearly enough the kinds of evil that attack the human body and mind with destructive consequences. These diseases arise from within the body and attack it in ways that it cannot overcome.

The final evil, inevitable for us all, comes at the end—death. Death is an evil. Paul spoke of it as "the last enemy to be destroyed" (1 Cor. 15:26). What lad, in the bright enthusiasm of youth, has not asked, "Why do I have to die?" Death, with its cold breath of finality, its final shattering of life's structures and meaning, comes to every friendship and family and eventually to each of us. Death issues the final challenge to every structure of meaning, challenging our final trust in the goodness of God and the ultimacy of the divine will.

These forms of evil do not visit us as strangers; they have been part of our awareness, if not our experience. None can escape their challenge to the meaning of life. I recall so well the bright and shining faces of John and Joan. Their lives had been changed in a lay renewal weekend; they were filled with joy and praise of God. He was a successful businessman in manufacturing and sales; she was a respected Bible teacher in her church. Periodically they flew together in their private plane to distant cities to share their newfound joy in Christ.

In a few years life changed radically. Joan began to develop trouble with her hip and had great difficulty walking; John Jr. went to Vietnam; Carol married and had a baby. During the last week of the war in Vietnam, John Jr. was killed. The day his body arrived in the city, his father filed for protection under the bankruptcy law because a trusted employee had embezzled several hundred thousand dollars.

In the wake of these multiple catastrophes Joan stopped teaching her Bible class; both ceased witnessing for Christ. Life had dealt them strike-out blows that drove meaning into eclipse. To protect themselves they withdrew. I'm sure they didn't want it that way, but it was the only way they saw to survive.

God's Will in the Face of Catastrophe

When catastrophes like these explode meaning, intuition seems lifeless and imagination frozen. How are such persons to affirm the will of God in the midst of their loss? Because the search for meaning has been identified with the search for the will of God, they are forced to ask, "How can we discern the will of God in the face of radical evil?"

Granted that these evils, sooner or later, challenge all of us with respect to God's will for lives, how do we discern the options open to us? We may question the goodness of God and come to doubt the existence of the divine purpose itself; we may turn with brutal self-criticism on ourselves, berating our failures and thereby heaping guilt on our heads; we may passively surrender to fate and with stoic composure accept the pain or loss; for a time we may escape through denial, pretending that the loss is unreal, or that by some miracle it will go away and, as those terrified by a nightmare, we will wake to discover that it was only a dream. Although people may deal with evil in their life experiences in one or all of these negative alternatives, none offers a way of creative discernment of God's will.

How shall we approach the dilemma? Maybe we will be aided by separating the negative aspects of these events. In the cases of the betrayal of a spouse, the senseless accident, and the failure of a business, human freedom shoulders blame. In human community, freedom provides a means of nurture and support, but this same relationship in community also exposes us to disappointment and sometimes harm. Each of these painful situations could have been avoided if the husband had chosen not to betray his wife's trust, the driver not to drink, the businessman not to make a speculative investment. In each instance the misuse of freedom played the major role, and thus its abuse explains the dilemma.

God did not will any of these catastrophes, but God has created the possibility of human freedom, and these destructive situations occurred through its misuse. When we are the victim of another's misuse of freedom, how do we discern the will of God?

The second series of events presents us with a different problem. Human freedom, expressed through ignorance or sin, seems to have no bearing on these occurrences. Violent eruptions of nature have traditionally been called "acts of God," and not just human freedom but also human involvement have been set aside. The destructive tremor of an earthquake, or the touching down of a tornado, or the blast of a hurricane against the coastline results in the destruction of cities and sometimes entire islands.

Again, these occurrences raise the question of the goodness and power of God. If God loves the world, how can God permit these calamities? At first glance the devastation caused by an earthquake might force us to conclude that either God does not care or God does not have the power to alter the situation. This conclusion, however, may not be the only way of phrasing the issue. Perhaps we will find a more appropriate question, but these forms of natural evil illustrate the occurrences of phenomena over which human beings have no control. Perhaps this lack of human initiative explains why they are called "acts of God."

In the third type of evil, nature seems vulnerable to the invasion of evil: cancer, Alzheimer's disease, and multiple sclerosis attack vital organs, the mind, the muscles. These and other diseases result in pain, the loss of bodily and mental functioning, dependency, and a life that is less than human. Illness deforms life, making it something other than God intended. These evils seem to arise from nature—the inadequacy, incompleteness, or vulnerability of nature.

Our discussion has made a distinction between evil originating in human freedom, the inexplainable destructiveness of nature, and the vulnerability of the human body. In the first instance we can attribute the destructive consequences of evil to the misuse of freedom. But even this abuse of God's gift could not occur unless God sustained life. In the case of illness, human freedom expressed in emotions may influence health. Psychosomatic research suggests that it does. And human beings are the subject of destruction caused by earthquakes and other forms of natural evil. Were it not for the vast destruction of human life, nature's eruptions would not so forcefully call attention to themselves. Yet when we have dealt with all these evils, we are still left with the specter of death.

Death, the Ultimate Threat

From one perspective, death is an evil. It ends life, separates people from their families and friends, often comes with great physical pain, and cannot be avoided. In another instance death may release people from pain and suffering. In either case, how are we to discern the will of God when death comes to those whom we love and, even closer, to each of us?

How can a person discern the will of God in these difficult situations? Our discussion suggests that we have difficulty enough discerning God's will under normal circumstances. Where do we look when the circumstances become questionable and disruptive? In order to begin plotting a positive course, we must begin with the disorientation that occurs through an encounter with radical evil. When evil strikes with its destruction, the intensity of our feeling varies with the proximity of the pain or the loss to us. The friends of the couple whose daughter was killed by a drunken driver, for example, could be incensed by the accident. But their feeling of disorientation and loss would never equal that of the parents. People like these parents, whose lives have been broken apart by radical evil, always suffer the greater loss—loss of family members, loss of dreams and hopes, loss of opportunity, loss of bodily functions. These losses produce grief, and grief early on eclipses purpose and meaning. When we can see no meaning it is difficult, if not impossible, to discern God's will.

The Stages of Grief

If the line from loss leads directly to grief, then the stages in the grief process suggest stages in the recovery of meaning. For our purpose the stages of grief provide different stages in the discernment of God's will.

The aspects of grief that erode meaning are shock, denial,

anger, blame, guilt, acceptance, and integration. These feelings form a spectrum of emotions in a situation of extreme loss. People may experience these feelings in different order, but all represent the destruction of meaning and thus of the positive awareness of God. We cannot feel these emotions associated with grief and sense the will of God at the same moment. Perhaps we can, through grace, voluntarily or volitionally affirm God's will, but we cannot experience the affirmation until we have done our grief work. An examination of these stages will illuminate our claim and point the way toward the recovery of meaning.

When the faithful wife discovers the betrayal of her husband her first reaction is shock. People in shock lose their orientation; they are blank, as if consciousness were erased for a moment. Shock is nature's anesthetic to assuage the pain of both physical and emotional injury.

In a state of shock, this wife does not discern the will of God; she is able to discern nothing because her consciousness is stuck in neutral. There is no recognition in shock. Shock also paralyzes the intuition; it does not flash impulses of a new future to the person in shock.

Next, grieving persons experience denial. What will the parents of the daughter killed in the wreck say when the shock wears off? "It's not true; tell me it's not true," they will cry. Denial, the second stage in the loss of meaning, attempts to keep the meaning of one's life intact. As long as the parents can deny the reality of the accident and the death of their daughter, they protect themselves against the abyss of meaninglessness and avoid the issue of God's will. Denial buys time, for a second or an hour; it gives space for the soul to adjust. Even the faintest hope—the reporter could be in error, it's a case of mistaken identity, she is not actually dead—makes space for the soul.

In denial these parents do not seek to discern the will of God in the evil that has taken their daughter; they don't require discernment as long as they can retain their present meaning and stability through denial.

The question of God's will becomes an issue only when

the reality of their loss has fully gripped them. Their first search for God begins with the question, "Why?" "Why?" introduces the subject of meaning and, ultimately, the question of God's will. Although this question may appear early in the negative experience, it does not dominate until much later. Like a cork on the troubled lake of conflicting emotions, this question surfaces, only to be submerged by the turbulent wind of doubt sweeping across the soul.

After denial comes anger. The man whose surgery revealed cancer responded with anger, fearful that life was ebbing. His anger may have been directed toward the doctor who informed him, his wife, himself, or even God. Whether in the beginning or later, he will probably turn his anger toward God as the cause of his loss. Anger defends against the ultimate threat to his life.

The question of "why?" soon disappears in the rage against the disease or God. Anger, unattended and unexpressed, turns to resentment. Long-term resentment erodes meaning and leads to bitterness and, eventually, despair.

In the stage of anger, the man who has learned of his cancer does not inquire into God's will; his energy expresses itself in anger. Although anger is an appropriate response to loss at an early stage, when it ripens into resentment and turns to bitterness, the soul has usually despaired of meaning and life has gone completely sour.

In the normal progression of grief, anger does not harden into lifelong resentment but turns to blame. In the case of the man who invested his life savings in a business that went bankrupt, in alternating moments he blamed his partner, his circumstances, and finally God for the bankruptcy. Blame is anger looking for reasons. Blame cannot positively affirm God's will; blame searches for a dumping ground for anger. The search for this garbage heap does not lead to the will of God, although it may clear the way for asking the question of God's will. Yet if a man full of blame met the will of God on the way to the garbage dump, he would not recognize it.

After blame comes guilt. Guilt is blame turned inward. When one feels guilty the most frequently uttered words are

"If I had only—" Guilt probably comes more sharply in instances of misused freedom: the wife blames herself for her husband's unfaithfulness; the parents blame themselves for permitting their daughter to leave that evening; the investor blames himself for his foolish choices.

Although guilt extended too long becomes an unhealthy self-pity or self-rejection, it does draw the person into the realm of selfhood where new decisions can be made. Guilt may soften the rebellion, preparing the way for acceptance.

The person feeling guilt, in respect to the will of God, sometimes takes the stance that the evil experienced has been a punishment for sin. This conclusion affirms God's will negatively. Guilt extended over a period of time leads to depression and, eventually, hopelessness.

All these stages of grief serve to screen consciousness from the perception and affirmation of God's will. One cannot embrace meaning when the circumstances of life have undercut the structure that has given it meaning. The experience of shock, the stance of denial, the feelings of anger, blame, and guilt, although normal, eclipse the positive sense of God's will. With the intuition paralyzed and the imagination frozen, the recovery of hope seems out of reach.

Although painful, these various aspects of the grief process occur in all of us who suffer loss. These stages can occur in sequence in a person's life. It may be that one person experiences only a few of these emotions, whereas another may have these negative feelings diluted with a strong faith; still another may have only slightly negative experiences. Whatever the depth of the negative experience, whenever we are gripped by these attitudes and feelings, which conflict so sharply with what we have identified as the will of God, we are tempted to despair of God's will. But maybe we should see this process not as a repudiation of God's will but as a manifestation of it. Perhaps these various stages offer us God's way of transition from one structure of the divine will to another. In transition, each stage offers respite to the soul that has been shaken to its core.

But on the other hand, to get stuck in any of these negative stages renders the will of God invisible to us. What attitude can we take when these evils come? First, it is important to feel what we feel; never deny feelings. In the second place, we can honestly state that we believe God can help us accept the loss, and also help to find the divine will. It would be a mistake to embrace the evil as the intention of God for us. This uncritical acceptance will serve as a shield against the pain we must feel, but it will not help us integrate the loss we have suffered.

This brings us to the two remaining stages of grief, acceptance and integration. By what means can we accept the negatives in life, and how can we integrate these into the ongoing narrative of meaning? Although we do not see the will of God clearly through our grief, we still believe it is there. And our concern is how do we pick up the trail again, when it is temporarily lost from sight?

Living through grief and loss of meaning is very much like flying on instruments. The pilot takes off on a bright, warm day. The trip progresses without incident until he encounters a thunderstorm. Dark, heavy clouds begin to sweep above, around, and beneath his plane. Only a few minutes before he could see the ground in fine detail, but now he sees nothing but clouds. At this point he must rely on his instruments to get him safely through the storm. The Christian, flying through dark clouds, must depend on the promises of God, the fellowship and support of friends, and the power of the worshiping community to see her or him safely through.

The Dimensions of God's Will

In some manner we must bring together the will of God and the devastation of radical evil. In the context of a gracious Creator whose ultimate will is our highest good, how can we relate this divine will to radical evil? Perhaps a few distinctions will help to sort out these two seemingly incompatible focuses. God's will has four dimensions: primal, provisional, permissive, and perfect.

The primal will points to God's original intention for creation and humanity. In the beginning, when the creative word brought the world into being, God said, "It is good!" In the good creation, God intended that freedom be realized within the divine purpose; that nature, created good, remain expressive of this divine intention; and that the good creation be invulnerable to disease, distortion, and death.

According to the biblical witness, the good creation was disrupted by the misuse of freedom, and the judgment of God ensued (Gen. 3:1–19). This view indicates that God's primal intention had been violated; human freedom became estranged from God's intention and God placed a curse on nature. In this frame of reference, the Fall violated but did not destroy the primal will of God. It perverted human freedom and left humankind vulnerable to disease and death. No evil had a place in God's original intention. In the tradition of Augustine, evil appears only as a parasite on the good. Evil has no separate ontological standing; it can exist only in dependence on the good.

Evil's entrance into human history gave occasion to God's provisional will. In the face of the violation of the primal will, the perversion of freedom, and the imperfection of nature, God still maintained a provisional purpose both for persons and for nature. Review God's primal will. Instead of this prehistory being the bliss of perfection, suppose it was the condition for development, both for a person and for nature. If humans had responded positively to God's primal will, if they had struggled in creation, they would have made God's will actual in history. Perhaps neither nature nor persons, although good, were complete at the beginning. Maybe God intended historical existence as the place of human becoming and nature's perfection. This view of reality recognizes struggle and growth as part of the primal intention.

When humans violated this primal intention, radical evil entered history by attacking nature at its vulnerable points and distorted its development. God's provisional will points to the presence of the divine intention in the context of perverted freedom and nature's abnormalities. Humans do use their freedom destructively, and nature does turn violent. But God appears in the midst of these evils, seeking good and pointing the way into the future.

In those instances of the misuse of freedom that resulted

in pain and destruction, God did not intend the loss, but in a provisional sense God supported human freedom and gave to nature its power. In a world in which freedom has substance and novelty exists as possibility, perhaps these abuses must be also a possibility. To debate whether this is the "best of all possible worlds" would be of no consequence because this is the only world that we have.

Next, in this less than perfect world, God has a permissive will. This aspect of God's will appears in Job, when God permitted Satan to test Job. The testing produced an attitude and maturity in Job that wealth, family, and success did not—nor could they. God does permit pain—physical and mental suffering, loss, disappointment, and fear—to call forth qualities in our lives that no other experience can produce. Can any of us deny that we have been most sensitive to God's will when our suffering was most intense?

God does not permit pain because of a delight in our suffering. God personally enters into our suffering and shares it; the incarnation makes God's participation abundantly clear. So, in our suffering, we can count on the unseen presence of God to sustain us until we see clearly to discern God's will.

Finally, God's perfect will, present now by anticipation, points ultimately to the perfection of persons and nature. In God's perfect will, maturity will have been achieved, history will have told its story, and all suffering, pain, and oppression will have been overcome. John must have had that vision when he wrote, "Then I saw a new heaven and a new earth; for the first heaven and the first earth had passed away, and the sea was no more" (Rev. 21:1).

In the meantime, what are we to do? We are to "believe in order that we may understand" because nothing comes to us apart from God's will—primal, provisional, permissive, or perfect. An encounter with radical evil interrupts the flow of our lives; it cuts into the narrative we have been telling and even calls it into question. Not until we accept the loss that comes to us can we go on with our story. The telling and retelling of our story, with confidence and meaning, permit the integration of pain into the meaning of our lives, or the discovery of the will of God for our lives.

Ten

Discerning the Will of God In and Through Community

This final exploration adds a corrective without which the individual search for the will of God would be perverted and nonproductive, if not destructive. The human perception and formulation of the will of God occurs in community. This brief excursion cannot exhaust the role of community in the task of discernment; it will not try to do so. To refocus the issues can, however, place the individual quest for God's will in the proper context; it can provide a vision of the quest in the larger context of history.

In the immeasurable past stands the Holy Trinity, who always shared the divine intention. The knowledge of this divine will, revealed in sacred history and clarified in the person of Christ, has been carried in the records, the traditions, and the memory of the people of God. For Christians, the church has always offered the context for discernment. From our perspective, the church could appropriately be called "the community of discernment." To place the issues we have raised in the proper relation, we will reflect on the individual spirit and its quest to discern the will of God, the church as a community of discernment, and the faculties of discernment as they relate to corporate discernment and the mission of the church.

136

The Individual Quest and Community

Thus far our discussion has taken place in the dialectic between the ultimate purposing God and the finite hunger and searching of the human spirit. This double search has the incarnate Christ as the norm for all discernment of God's will. Because all creation, including the human soul, came into being through the word of God (John 1:1–5), it has been stamped with the divine image and will. Although estranged from the divine will through sin, the thin tracings of the will of God still lie on the darkened soul. The faculties of the soul, although damaged, still have the capacity to formulate a notion of the divine will. These capacities include reason, which receives images from intuitions, shapes them by the power of creative imagination, and appeals to the will that acts out the chosen images.

The soul also has the capacity to recall; it can bring into the present events of the past to review the ways of God, an act that both influences present decisions and deepens wisdom. These affirmations presuppose the Christian community and depend on it in creating and shaping an individual's life. But we have not specified the dangers of a private search for the will of God, a search outside the larger community of faith. What pitfalls await the person who resists participation in the community of faith?

Perhaps we should begin with individualism—an egoism gone to seed in which a person has become convinced that she or he can go it alone. In this country we have inherited John Locke's brand of individualism in which the individual precedes the community and the community comes into existence through the voluntary contract of individuals. This notion, which was fundamental in the founding of the republic, has also influenced how people see the church. But the church is not the result of a social contract voluntarily agreed on by a collection of individuals; the church is a community called and created by God. It has its reality in God's will and not the contract of self-seeking, self-sufficient individuals.

Who has not met the man or woman who, disillusioned

with the church, says, "I have Jesus and the Bible—that's all I need to find and do God's will." This stalwart, self-confident soul retreats from the community of faith to read the Bible and through the Spirit privately discern the will of God. Soon this sincere but deluded seeker hears nothing but echoes bouncing about in his or her head. The discernment of the will of God is personal but not private.

Even if the solitary individual accurately discerns God's will, where will support come from to do God's bidding? The most resolute disciple eventually grows weary and withdraws from the fray unless voices of affirmation support and confirm the call of God. The discernment of the will of God requires support.

If our solitary figure could imagine the will of God and define a course of action, what will protect him or her from perversion? At best, our decisions are ambiguous and our actions incomplete, but left to ourselves we are exceedingly vulnerable to selfish egoistic perversion. Does not this sincere but misguided soul need an objective voice, someone to speak and refine his or her perceptions? Without these correctives from the outside, the opportunities for self-deception multiply. The search for the will of God requires a community to serve as a corrective voice.

For the committed Christian, a private quest faces yet another difficulty. By its very nature, Christianity requires others; it requires community. At the heart of Jesus' teachings stands the commandment, "You shall love the Lord your God with all your heart, and with all your soul, and with all your mind. . . . You shall love your neighbor as yourself" (Matt. 22:37, 39). How can a person love those with whom she or he has no relation? To love God and to love the neighbor takes persons out of isolation into relationship and thus into community. A private quest denies the very heart of the faith.

The solitary individual, without roots in a community, faces another common and pervasive malady—amnesia. Perhaps no other force operates to destroy the individual quest so effectively. Human beings—all human beings—forget! We forget who we are! Where we have been! What we are to do! But by participation in the community of faith, we are continually reminded by tradition and the liturgy of the decisive events in our Christian history. The memory of the community existed before us; it called forth our faith; it has sustained us and given direction to life. To withdraw from the community severs us from this historical grounding.

If the quest for the will of God has this strong communal dimension, the church must become a community of discernment. No disappointment will be greater to a serious seeker for God's will than to enter a church seeking bread and be given a stone. The vitality of its corporate life, the authenticity of its members' lives, and the sensitivity that they have to those who earnestly inquire of the will of God—all these features signal the effectiveness of a particular church in helping persons find God's will.

The Church: A Discerning Community

Having established the necessity of community for the person who would discern God's will, we must inquire into the ways the church provides a context for discernment. The church has a long history and a deep memory; it has nearly 2,000 years of its own, plus another 1,500 years of Jewish history from which to draw insights. This collective consciousness of the people of God provides an accumulation of wisdom greater than a thousand lifetimes. In this vast memory, every conceivable issue has been faced by the human family.

Perhaps the major issues described in this long story relate to meaning, how persons are to live—that is, the will of God for humankind. The church of Jesus Christ, a contemporary expression of God's people, holds in its corporate memory the decisions, failures, judgments, pardon, and restoration of God's people. But the church is more; it is the body of Christ. Karl Barth describes it as "the earthly form of his existence." As the community of Christ, it is the bearer of his presence on earth. Because Christ enfleshes the will of God, to say that the the church is therefore the concrete expression of the will of God would be logical but not correct; it is the bearer of his will but not the concrete, perfect manifestation of that divine intention.

As a bearer of God's will, the church has the word and sacrament. The word continues to witness to the will of God; it contains the voice of Christ, which comes against us, limits us, and corrects us. This word addresses us, shattering our isolation and correcting our delusions. That word also comes to us with forgiveness, speaking healing when we fail to do God's will. Therefore, the word is a lamp to our feet and a light to our path (see Ps. 119:105).

The church has the sacraments: baptism and the Lord's Supper. One initiates us into the community and the other sustains us on our journey. Baptism, as a rite of initiation, incorporates us into his body; it speaks of our consciously beginning to participate in the community that bears God's intention. Baptism, linking us to others in the body of Christ, denies privatism and every form of individualism; it signifies our union with Christ and with every person who names Jesus Christ as Lord.

The bread and the wine nourish faith and symbolize the internalization of God's will. As one of the ancients has said, "We become the body of Christ when we partake of the body of Christ." This sacramental worship unites us believers with Christ, making our lives an expression of the divine will.

The celebration of the Eucharist provides an anamnesis— a recalling of the past and making it present. Each time the bread is broken and the wine poured, the participants remember; this act breaks through our amnesia, calling us to an awareness of Christ.

Through word and sacrament, the presence of Christ comes to us, addresses us, and sustains us. As Presence, Christ empowers us to discern God's will and form its expressions through our choices. Isolated individuals cannot live in the will of God without the sustaining and directing power of the community.

The church also, by its very nature as a community, provides "a sacred canopy," a tent of meaning that defines reality. Without the shared vision of reality, reinforced through worship and fellowship, the individual soul loses its grasp on the vision of God's intention for humanity. The church is at once a social institution and a divine reality.

Each service of worship presupposes and reinforces this sacred order. Think about the "sacred canopy," the picture of reality the liturgy evokes. The call to worship invites us into the presence of the holy God, one who knows us and can be approached by us. In worship we offer praise to God! Praise suggests the awesome, mysterious dimension of the divinely inhabited cosmos. With a little imagination, anyone can see the world created by the other elements of worship: prayers of confession acknowledge a moral universe; prayers of the people, a benevolent God who responds to human need; sermons, the voice of God speaking in contemporary form; an offering, the consecration of life to God.

Worship keeps this structure of reality intact and provides a context of meaning for believers. Only within this framework can faithful Christian discernment occur. Regular corporate worship affirms the Christian vision of the world. Without participation in this community, the experiences of life have a way of ripping the canopy and exposing the lone individual to meaninglessness and despair.

The private quest for discernment has numerous pitfalls, and the community of faith provides a storied context, a norm, and a shared vision of reality that address the dilemma of the individual. These gifts of community present themselves through fellowship with others who know the story, who incarnate the presence of Christ, and who share the vision of the sacred. Our fellowship with other believers mediates the benefits of the community to us.

But more specifically, regarding discernment, this fellowship not only informs us but also serves to free us from our illusions, support us in transitions, remind us of who we are, and present us with concrete manifestations of love.

Certain ones of the brothers and sisters will become the eyes and ears of Christ, viewing our expression of his will and hearing our confession when we fail. This community also holds within its memory the stories and teachings of Jesus, a contemporary expression of the mind of Christ. And these embodiments of the divine presence speak the word of Christ, in both an affirmative and a corrective way.

In skepticism, some people may exclaim that they have never experienced such intimacy with the divine will in the church. The answer may lie in not having looked for the living expression of Christ in the community, or in the indifference of believers to the divine presence within them. Whether manifest or not, the Lord Christ intends his body to be a community of discernment so that God's kingdom may come and God's will be done on earth as it is in heaven.

Discernment and History

Reference to the will of God being done on earth, as it is in heaven, introduces yet another aspect of this community's life. Not only does the church provide a corrective to individualism as a corporate expression of Christ, but as a community of discernment it aims to recognize the will of God in history. Discernment of the will of God for the individual always stands within the larger task of discerning the will of God for all of life. What the human spirit seeks for the individual, the spirit of the church seeks for society. In this sense, the church is the soul of society.

The idea of the spirit of a church can be noted in every congregation. When we describe a church as being dead or alive, those words evoke images in our minds—warm and cold call up contrasting images—and these words have meaning with respect to the corporate life of a congregation. Although the concept of spirit can be slippery to define, I intend it to signify the life principle of a corporate community.

The Spirit of the Church

The spirit of the church possesses two aspects, the objective and the subjective. The objective spirit of the church contains the values, dreams, experiences, and failures of the culture of its members. This complex corporate spirit has many facets that refuse to be neatly labeled, but at its center it expresses the corporate incarnation of the Spirit in a particular culture. If a particular congregation is the incarnation of the Spirit in a local culture, perhaps a denomination is the corporate expression of all its member churches.

The structures of the church provide the framework for carrying this Spirit. It is not identified with these structures, but they provide the form though which it expresses itself. In the Presbyterian Church (U.S.A.), for example, the Spirit revealing the will of God works through the sessions of particular congregations, but the Spirit also acts through the collective mind of presbytery, synod, and General Assembly. The difficulty arises when those who speak for the denomination do not accurately represent the congregations that constitute it. This difference in bureaucratic vision and grass-roots action characterizes not only the Presbyterian Church but all denominations.

The mission in which a particular church engages is a fleshing out of this corporate spirit. These activities re-present Christ in contemporary form.

The objective spirit is the human side of the church's life as it expresses itself incarnationally in a particular culture. This spirit is ambiguous and incomplete.

The church also has a subjective spirit. We might also call this aspect of the spirit the collective memory of the church. In this memory resides the image of Christ—incarnate, crucified, and risen. He is the church's spiritual essence, seeking to express himself in the essential marks of unity, holiness, apostolicity, and universality. This subjective spirit also expresses itself in the tasks of worship, nurture, service, and witness. Perhaps this vision justifies our speaking of the church as "his earthly form of existence." The risen Christ is not identical with the subjective spirit of the church, yet his image informs, empowers, and directs it.

This informing role of the subjective spirit gives direction to the church. This dimension of the subjective spirit propels the church in its mission and seeks to form it according to the image of Christ. This presence of Christ in the depth of the community points to the dynamic aspect of the church's mission.

This subjective spirit also contains the collective wisdom of the church. This wisdom, gathered through the centuries, provides images of the corporate expression of Christ. In fulfilling its apostolate to the world, the church has grown in stature, knowledge, and wisdom in the ways of God on this earth. Becoming open to this collective wisdom enables the church to act with faithfulness.

Finally, the Holy Spirit impinges on the subjective spirit of the church. The Holy Spirit, though never identical with the subjective spirit, acts on this depth dimension of the community's life, resurrecting the image of Christ, driving the church into the world, and calling forth the collective wisdom of the community.

These two aspects of the church's spirit, though distinguishable, cannot be separated. The subjective and objective unite to express the corporate life of the church, and the history of worship and ministry resides in the corporate memory of the community as a narrative. This developing narrative contains the church's identity; it provides continuity within a particular church's life and becomes a unique, contemporary expression of the longer tradition to which it belongs.

At this point the issue of discernment becomes crucial. The dynamic essence of the church, stimulated by the Holy Spirit, joins with the values, dreams, and needs of a particular community of people to incarnate Christ. Corporate discernment demands that the community, inhabited by the presence of Christ, express the will of God in a particular historical situation. These concrete manifestations of the earthly form of Christ suffer all the ambiguities of the individual effort to do the will of God. Apparently no other option is available in the condition of fallenness.

Faculties for Discernment in the Community

What faculties for discernment are accessible to the corporate community? Can we claim that those aspects of discernment available to individuals exist in the community in a corporate form? A speculative discussion of these faculties as resources of the corporate consciousness provides a perspective on the realization of the church as a community of discernment. These corporate faculties include the core desire within the church, the corporate intuition, imagination, historical memory, and the risk of doing the will of God.

The dynamic drive to re-present Christ to the world in visible form receives its impetus from the image of Christ in the subjective spirit of the church. The church, the body of Christ, exists to express this essential nature in specific historical form. This dynamic energy, however, must combine with the objective spirit with all its historical and cultural influences. To ignore or repudiate this essential reason for the church's being is to abandon its vocation. (Recall our assertion that God wills to become flesh.) Interaction of the subjective and objective spirit contributes the dynamic and formal aspects of the will of God being made flesh in a historical setting.

How, then, can a particular congregation discern the will of God in order to engage in its mission? There are three dynamic elements in its life: (1) the context of the subjective spirit, where it exists; (2) its reason for being, an earthly form of Christ; and (3) the content of the objective spirit, the culture of the members. To discern God's will means to discern what God intends for this particular community in its historical setting.

We now ask, "How does the body of Christ discern the will of God for its corporate life?" The first step in corporate discernment of the will of God is the church's desire to do God's will, a fundamental shift in perspective from fulfilling its own will. The church does not exist for itself but for the will of God. The congregation that does not live in this essential awareness will never, ever, inquire into the will of God.

Second, the data for discernment emerge from the corporate consciousness of the congregation. Practically speaking, each member (or at least a representative number) must be given opportunity to reflect on the question "What does God will for us to do in our particular context?" This question draws on the intuitions, creative imaginations, and collective memory of the body of Christ. This serious inquiry also opens the consciousness of the congregation to the presence of the Holy Spirit. Responses to this inquiry into the will of God will sort themselves out. The collective wisdom of the congregation that emerges through dialogue will enable it to prioritize dreams and hopes and to formulate its perception of the divine intention.

In this process the congregation must never forget that its formulations of the divine will have been conditioned by its shared vision, values, and history. The will of God cannot be made actual except by conditioned, limited vision. Therefore, the church should never think that its decisions are exempt from the judgment of God. In all our striving to discern God's will, the sovereign, gracious God acts in ways we do not understand and achieves the divine intention in spite of human sin and willfulness.

I am aware that this description of the spirit of a church has been theoretical and highly abstract. A natural question arises: What does it look like when a particular church incarnates the will of God in its cultural life?

Once I was involved with a rather large church during a long-range planning process. The leadership of the church gathered data from members of the congregation that expressed their visions and concerns for the church; the committee also obtained all the demographic information about the community. This information was presented to the session, or governing body, of the church. With those data the leaders asked, "What is God calling us to be and do in this location at this time in our history?" In response to this query came specific tasks that members of this particular church thought they had to undertake. In other words, they engaged in a corporate enterprise of discernment. The leaders believed that their decisions were an effort to incarnate the will of God in the world.

I live with the dream that the whole church will become self-conscious in listening to the call of God in the context of its life. When the church begins listening, it will be informed by the image of Christ, its memory, and the frequent initiatives of the Holy Spirit. Obedience to this calling will be a concrete, though ambiguous, embodiment of the will of God in history.

The Dream

When I had finished the description of the church as a community of discernment, a dream came to me—not a night dream or a daydream but what I would call a life dream.

In my dream I found myself in a strange city. I wandered around for a long time, and when finally it occurred to me that I was lost, the awareness struck a note of terror inside me. I began to walk faster and faster until my pace became a jog.

After a while, tired and exhausted, I sat down on the steps of a rough gray-stone building. Suddenly I heard music—joyful, rather loud music with a rhythmic beat. A choir of voices filled the air with a melody that magnetically drew me inside.

As I began the long climb up three flights of steps, I looked up. High above me in the center of this building I saw a multicolored mosaic of Christ standing with outstretched arms. Beneath the image of Christ was written, *Come unto me all you that labor and are heavy laden.*

The music, the architecture, and the mosaic all told me that I was entering a church. Once inside, I began to assess the gathering. People sat in folding chairs all the way down the aisles, so packed was the room. Most of the worshipers could not have been a day over forty-five; many were younger.

What impressed me most was the joy they seemed to experience—glowing faces, broad smiles, bodies swaying, hands clapping. Their worship had the atmosphere of a party, a God party.

If anything impressed me more than the singing and joy, it was the spirit. An invisible, warm, magnetic presence pervaded the service. Through the singing and clapping and swaying, this spirit drew me into the group. I found myself a part of the community without a word ever being spoken. As I began to give myself to the spirit, a young brunette about twenty looked up at me with a knowing twinkle in her eye.

The music stopped. The crowd sat down. I began to take

inventory—a choir of one hundred, a twenty-piece orchestra, perhaps a thousand excited people. Over the choir stretched a banner that read, *A Community of Discernment*.

A man dressed in a dark business suit rose, opened the Bible, and read from First Corinthians, "As it is written . . . eye has not seen." Then he began to speak. His words had no dramatic flair; they were simple, direct, from the heart, from God. He declared that Christ had a purpose for every life, that Christ would reveal his purpose to anyone who would listen. He concluded with the statement, "As the body of Christ, we are a community of discernment and thus offer ourselves to you to help you find your way."

At the conclusion of the service twenty-five to thirty persons made their way to the front to talk with the elders. I felt an attraction myself.

Before I could move, the young man to my right inquired if I'd like to join his group for a drink or something to eat. The invitation came with such warmth and sincerity that I couldn't refuse.

We made our way down the street to a small restaurant. While waiting for the food, I asked, "How would you describe this church?"

"Oh, it's a community of Christ," he said.

"And how did you get there?"

"A friend. I saw such an amazing transformation in her. I decided to investigate."

"And?"

"And I came here with no knowledge of God, no sense of direction in life, no goals, no firm values."

"So?"

"So I experienced the same Presence that you did tonight. I went forward for counseling."

"Tell me how you found meaning for your life."

"After my initial response, I was assigned a sponsor; he answered the questions that arose about God. Then I became part of a discernment group that helped me review my life from this new faith perspective. I got an image of my future through intuition, prayer, imagination, and meditation."

"Sounds like a group that takes God seriously."

"You haven't heard the half of it. This whole church is like that."

"How would you describe this church?"

"It is the body of Christ, a community of discernment intent on doing his will on earth as it is done in heaven."

Have you ever had a dream that you hoped would never end? But then you wake up to reality. Yet in some ways you can never be the same because you "saw," as in a dream, a vision of how things ought to be!

What is that quote?

"Some look at things as they are and ask, 'Why?' Others dream of how things ought to be and ask, 'Why not?' "[12]

Appendix A

Reflection Exercises

This book will be most profitable to people who are struggling with an issue of discernment. Spiritual guides will be aided by applying these insights to their lives. Authentic discipleship grows out of an experiential base called for by these exercises.

The use of a journal provides a convenient and permanent place to work through the exercises and record your insights. Each chapter adds a new dimension to the task of discernment; the exercises provide guidance in personal application. Read the chapter and then do the exercises.

Chapter 1: The Search for Meaning

1. Describe a current issue in your life in which you need discernment. Answering these questions will help: What is the issue? From what circumstances does it emerge? Who else will be affected by your decisions? Why does this issue seem important to you?

2. In short paragraphs write a brief history of your search for the meaning of your life. Reflect on how the current issue is a continuation of that search.

3. Review the narrative of your search for meaning and write a prayer of thanksgiving for hungers felt and grace given.

4. Review the description of the current issue in your life in which you need discernment. Make changes or clarifications as a result of your review.

Chapter 2: The Will of God

This exercise intends to help you relate your faith to your experience of the will of God. State how each element in the Apostles' Creed relates to discerning and doing the will of God. For example, take the affirmation "I believe in God the Father Almighty." You might relate to this affirmation by stating, "I believe that God has a will for my life, that God's will is more important than my will, that God's will ultimately will prevail."

Respond to each sentence below in this manner and write as long as ideas bubble up in your mind.

1. I believe in God the Father Almighty.
2. I believe in Jesus Christ, God's Son.
3. I believe in the Holy Spirit.
4. I believe in the church of Christ.
5. I believe in the forgiveness of sins.
6. I believe in the resurrection of the body.
7. I believe in the life everlasting.

Review each of the statements you have made regarding your faith as it relates to God's intention for your life. Note the kind of faith perspective from which you view this issue. Is God friendly to your search? Accessible to you?

Chapter 3: The Will of God Made Flesh

Use this outline of the will of God as manifest in Christ to review Christ's life and teachings as the norm for God's will.

As you review these ideas, note those that seem to relate to your particular issue. This outline will help you recall the text. How does the manifestation of God's will in Christ inform your issue? Do the life and teachings of Christ challenge the faith perspective described in the previous exercise?

All references are from the Gospel of John.

I.   The identification of Christ with the will of God

   1:1–5   The word Christ was with God and was God.

   1:14   Christ as the will of God was made flesh.

   1:18   No one has ever seen God, but Christ made flesh has made God known.

   3:34   Christ who was with God speaks the word of God to us.

   12:44   The person who believes in Christ believes not only in him but in God who sent him.

   14:6   Whoever has seen Christ has seen the nature of God.

   17:26   Christ made God's name and nature and will known to us.

II. The mode of God's will coming to us in Christ

   5:2–10   The will of God cannot be contained fully in laws and commandments. Jesus broke the law of the Sabbath to express love to one who was sick.

   5:30–47   The sources of discernment for us are the works we do, the witness of another, God's witness to us, and the witness of scripture.

   6:50–56   The will of God comes through eating the flesh and drinking the blood of Jesus Christ. The sacrament internalizes the will of God.

   9:29   One can be confident of the tradition but uncertain of Christ, so that the tradition blinds one to the living Christ.

   13:5   The will of God comes to us as a servant.

14:17   The Spirit of Christ dwells within us, teaching us the will of God.

14:22–23 As indwelling presence, Christ guides us.

15:26   The Spirit within serves as a witness to Christ.

16:7–11   The Spirit reproves the world when it fails to keep God's will.

16:13–15 The Spirit guides us into all the truth about Christ.

III. The metaphors Christ used that illuminate aspects of the will of God he manifests

6:35   The will of God is the bread of life that sustains us.

8:12   The will of God is the light of the world that illuminates our pathway.

10:1–6   The will of God is a shepherd who knows, leads, and protects us.

10:10   The will of God is a door providing openings to new possibilities and closure on old history.

11:9–10; The will of God is made apparent through light and
12:35–36 obscured through darkness.

12:46   The will of God is a light that has come into the world that we should not live and walk in darkness.

14:6   The will of God is the way, the truth, and the life for all of us.

15:1–7   The will of God is a vine on which all of us depend for nourishment and strength.

16:20–28 When the will of God is ignored or forgotten, it creates travail like a woman giving birth to a child.

IV. The content of the will of God expressed by Christ

3:7   Spiritual birth is necessary to recognize and do the will of God.

4:46–54 An encounter with the centurion shows that it is God's will to heal the sick and relieve anxiety.

6:16–21   The will of God comes to us in our distress as Christ came to the struggling disciples on the sea.

6:37–40   Those whom God has given to Christ will come to Christ. They will not be lost but will have eternal life.

13:12–15 Christ gave us an example that we should serve others as he served us.

21:15   Love is the content of God's will. He continually asks, "Do you love me?"

V.   Various responses to God's will

6:60   At times the disciples murmured against God's will, saying, "It is a hard saying."

7:6   The response comes at the proper time. At one junction his time had not come, but when the proper time came, he was manifest. So it is with the will of God.

7:12   The will of God in us draws opposing responses. Some say, "We're crazy." Others say, "We are good people."

7:17   The best response to God's will is to will God's will.

7:20   Some will say we have a demon.

7:46   People will often recognize that we are speaking in a different tone: that is, with an internal authority.

12:24–26 To receive the will of God is like a grain of wheat that falls into the earth and dies. Though it sacrifices itself, it rises and reproduces.

13:31–32 Jesus viewed the betrayal by Judas as his being glorified and as part of God's will for him.

16:1–4   We will be treated with contempt by those who do not know God or care for God's will.

16:26–28 Jesus embraced the will of God, knowing that it led to his death.

18:17   Some will deny they know the will of God.

18:11   Others embrace the will of God as their cup to drink.

VI. Consequences of encountering God's will

  3:36   Believing and receiving God's will brings life.

  4:31–34   Doing God's will gives food that others do not know about. It provides satisfaction.

  5:10–18   To claim God's will evokes hostility from the religious establishment.

  7:36   Some will seek Christ but will not find him. Rejection of Christ hides the will of God from us.

  8:29   Those who receive the will of God live a life that pleases God.

  8:32   Those who do the will of God will be made free.

  9:25   Those who embrace the will of God know that once they were blind but now they see.

  12:24–26 Those who grasp God's will are like grains of wheat. Self-realization comes through self-sacrifice.

  14:27   Peace is given to those who do God's will.

  15:11   Christ has bequeathed his joy to those who do God's will.

  18:23–24 The will of God gives courage to challenge the authority.

VII. The style of God's will

  1:39   It invites us to explore. It says, "Come and see."

  2:23–25   On occasion, it withholds itself from us when it knows we are unprepared for it.

  3:17   The will of God never comes to condemn us, but to affirm and liberate us.

Chapter 4: The Will of God Written in the Soul

In ways unknown, God's will has been written in the structure of our being. This will has made its appearance to our minds in a variety of ways and through the years has received different responses.

1. Think back over your life. What dream has repeatedly come to you regarding your life? Write a brief description.

2. Name the various circumstances in which this dream for your life has come to your awareness.

3. Identify the various responses you have made to this dream. Under what circumstances did you make these responses?

4. What major obstacles have you encountered in pursuing this dream?

5. What disappointments have you experienced?

6. How does this dream for your life relate to the issue of discernment you now face?

7. What observations do you make about the dream that you hold for your life and the manner in which you have sought to fulfill it?

Chapter 5: Intuition: A Source of Discernment

The following instructions will help you to create a friendly environment for your intuitions. You may want to record them on a tape player so you may be guided through the process without having to open your eyes. After each suggestion, pause for a minute and do it.

Get comfortably seated. Relax.

Begin at your head, picturing all the tension draining out of your head, face, and neck, flowing over your shoulders and down through your arms, and dripping out of your fingertips.

Continue the relaxation exercise, inch by inch, until you have relaxed every muscle to the tips of your toes.

In this relaxed, meditative mood hold in front of your mind an image of the issue you are dealing with. Think of the issue as a magnet that draws images, ideas, and inspirations from your unconscious depths.

Do not force the process. Adopt a receptive mode of consciousness. Let your deeper self speak. You are more likely to have images and feelings than you are to have verbal messages.

Write down the images that begin coming to you. As you begin to write, each thought will attach itself to another, pulling it up. Writing serves as a rope that draws ideas and images from your depths.

Keep at this receptive writing for as long as the inspiration lasts. If the images cease, you may pause, become quiet, and listen. More may come. At some point you will have a sense of having completed listening for the time being.

When you have finished writing, read over what you have written. How does it connect with the issue of discernment with which you are struggling? Note any insights that have come to you from your intuition. Ask yourself these questions:

1. What new options do I see regarding the issue?
2. Which of these options have a sense of rightness about them?
3. Do my intuitions suggest changes that I personally need to make in either attitude or behavior?
4. Are other people involved? How will my decisions affect them?
5. Do any of my intuitions have a feeling of freshness and creativeness about them?

Chapter 6: Imagination and Discernment

The imagination works closely with intuition, but in some instances it performs its tasks separately and under more direct, conscious control. In this exercise we will build on the intuition recorded from the exercise for chapter 5 and take a creative step beyond the images produced by intuition.

1. Review the images received from your intuition in the preceding exercise.

2. Expand each of these images through meditation. To expand the idea, hold it in your mind; repeat it softly to yourself; be silent. Record the new ideas and images that cluster around the subject of your meditation.

3. Expand each of these ideas further by engaging it in dialogue. Think of the image or idea as a person. Ask questions of it. Write what you think the image or idea would say. Respond to what you have written. Continue the dialogue as long as inspiration comes to you.

4. From the various ideas that have come to you through intuition, meditation, and imagination choose the three that have the strongest appeal to you. In your journal write what you imagine would be the consequences of each of the choices.

5. To this point you have built imaginatively on your intuitions. Take a break of an hour or even a day before coming back to the subject. Permit the work you have already done to settle into your psyche.

6. Review the issue for which you are seeking discernment. In the power of your creative imagination create three desirable futures. In narrative form, write these futures as a scenario. To write a scenario, imagine that you are ten years into the future: where are you, what are you doing, how did you get there, what is happening as a consequence, how do you feel about your situation?

7. Which of these scenarios would you most like to come to pass? Why? Which seems to be expressive of the will of God for you? (Review the exercise for chapter 3, "The Will of God Made Flesh," to refresh your evaluative powers.)

8. Review the futures that you projected from the data of your intuition. How do these futures compare?

Chapter 7: Discernment Through Memory

The first step in discerning the will of God in our history requires that we begin with the centers of meaning in our lives. Identify those centers in your life. (This exercise has also been included in chapter 7 to illustrate the discussion there.) Each of these probably holds common themes, or threads of meaning. To ferret out these threads, begin with the current era of your life and answer these questions about it and each center:

1. When did this era begin?
2. What was the setting geographically? In the larger society?
3. Who were the significant persons?
4. What gifts did the setting evoke? What potential did it actualize?
5. What feelings—emotional responses—most often accompanied the occurrences?

6. How was God at work in these persons and events? What especially did God seem to be doing through you?
7. What were the dominant threads, or trends, in the center? What are their roots in the past? Their possible expressions in the future?
8. What are your feelings about the closing of the era? Muse over these insights and pay attention to the intuitions they inspire for the future.

When you have finished reflecting on your centers of meaning, ask your deeper self for a symbol of your life. I suspect that the symbol will manifest itself in all the centers of meaning, and it too is predictive for your future. The symbol or image to which I have always been attracted is the "explorer."

Chapter 8: Doing the Will of God

Discernment of God's will comes in part from doing God's will. Assurance of the will of God most often comes in retrospect, but discernment gives both courage and direction in taking the next step. This exercise aims to help you test your intuitions and images of God's will for you and to take the initial steps of obedience.

1. As clearly as you can, state what you believe to be God's will regarding your issue. (If new issues have surfaced in your reflections, stay with the first issue for now.)

2. If this is God's will for you, are you willing to do it?

3. Test this perception of God's will by the following internal factors:

Did it come to you in gentleness?
Is the guidance clear?
Are the first steps specific?
Does this direction have a convictional character?
Does the guidance persist? Does it repeatedly come to your mind?
Are you at peace with this guidance?

4. Test your perception by the following external factors:

Do any other people confirm your understanding of God's will
    for you regarding this issue?
If you obey God in this way, will your behavior exemplify the
    Spirit of Christ?
As you reflect on the character of Christ, does the sense of God's
    will fit with the spirit, style, and content of the revelation
    of God in Christ?
Does this course of action accord with the tenor of scripture as
    you understand God's revelation?

5. Will you choose to do the will of God as you understand
it? What will be the first three actions you take to enact God's
will for you?
6. With whom will you share these decisions to make yourself accountable to that person?
7. Live into your obedience.

Chapter 9: The Will of God and the Problem of Evil

The purpose of this exercise is to help you begin sorting
out your life when you have experienced a trauma that results
in feelings of meaninglessness. If you have not healed suffi-
ciently to begin the process, do not be discouraged. Lay the
guidelines down until such time as you have the energy to
begin the work of reconstruction.
1. Describe the traumatic situation of loss as fully as you
can. Include a description of your feelings of disappointment,
pain, fear, anger. Don't edit your feelings. Write about all the
feelings that surface.
2. How would you classify the situation: a misuse of freedom, a miscue of nature, an attack on nature, death?
3. Describe your experience of the following:

Shock
Denial
Anger
Blame—God, self, others

Guilt
Acceptance
Integration

4. At what stage are you in the process of dealing with the presence of radical evil in your life? Do you feel stuck?

5. Write a short essay in which you express your desire for God's will and your deepest feelings about the manner in which God has dealt with you.

6. Which aspect of God's will seems to apply to your situation?

God's primal will: What aspect of this problem betrays God's original intention?

God's provisional will: Has someone misused the created freedom God gave to all? Has grace been provided in the midst of gross evil?

God's permissive will: Has God permitted this evil for some purpose? What are possible constructive purposes in your loss?

God's perfect will: In time or beyond, imagine the perfect solution to your loss. Is it possible? Can you believe that in history or beyond history a just and gracious God will rectify this loss?

7. Integrate the evil, or loss, into the narrative of your life. (The choice we do not have is that of turning back time and making the situation other than what it is. Loss is real, painful, and irrevocable.)

What part of your history has been attacked? Describe it.

Stand firmly in the awareness of the loss. What faint intuitions do you have about the future? When intuitions are paralyzed, or speak with a weak voice, listen and grasp each firmly.

Expand your strongest and most positive intuitions into a scenario—an imagined future—that will give you a reason for living.

Name the first three steps that will begin your journey beyond tragedy.

8. What do you think God wills for you?

Prayers in Grief
Shock: O God, I can't pray.
Denial: Lord God, this has not happened.
Anger: I hate you, God, and never want to think of you again.
Blame: Why, O God, did you do this to me?
Guilt: What did I do wrong, Lord?
Acceptance: Thy will be done, thy kingdom come.
Integration: Thank you for a new future.

9. Permit the Spirit of God to mediate a reconciliation between the opposites in your life: a good God and evil facts; expectations and reality; a flow of meaning and an abyss that swallows all meaning.

10. Bring your hurt into a community of faith. Let yourself be sustained by those who believe there is meaning even when you cannot.

Chapter 10: Discerning the Will of God In and Through Community

How can the church discern the will of God for society? How can it be the soul of history with its corporate memory, intuitions, imagination, and actions? This process is for ministers, elders, and committee members.

1. The church, "the earthly form of his existence," has as its mission to do corporately what Jesus did personally in the flesh. Review the metaphors, modes, content, and consequences of the will of God manifest in Jesus. (See the exercise for chapter 3.)

2. What aspect of the mission of Christ—worship, nurture, compassion, justice, outreach—does this effort represent?

3. Memory: In what ways have we expressed this aspect of Christ's person in the past? How has this performance expressed or betrayed his will?

4. What practices or attitudes in society violate this intention of Jesus Christ?

5. Intuition: Given our current circumstance, what new focus might the will of Christ take in our midst?

6. Imagination: Envision a new order, a new scenario, for society in which this evil has been overcome.

7. What specific action can be taken to place in motion the will of Christ in our situation?

Appendix B

An Abbreviated Exercise in Discernment

After reading this text on discernment, you may not have performed each of the exercises but may wish to work on a specific issue in your life. Use this short form to focus on the issue and seek guidance. Follow each of these steps, using a journal to record your work.

Phase I: Description
Describe the issue in your life. Elaborate the choice that must be made, the feelings you have, the depth of your desire to do God's will.

Phase II: The Norm in Jesus
Read the statements about the norm in Jesus (see the exercise for chapter 3 in Appendix A).

What does the content of God's will say to you about this issue?

Which of the metaphors of Jesus holds promise—bread, light, door, servant, way, truth, life?

State how the metaphors connect with your issue.

Review the statements concerning the mode of God's will

164

as a refresher before engaging other faculties of the soul. How do you expect God's will to come to you in this issue?

Phase III: Intuitions
State your intuitions about the will of God in this situation.

Become quiet and let your consciousness be open to your depths. Permit images to float freely.

Write down the images that flow through your mind. Identify the numerous perceptions, feelings, and ideas about the issue.

Which of these intuitions has kinship, or the closest kinship, with the content of Christ's will?

Do these intuitions have the positive consciousness that God's will produces?

Prioritize these intuitions after having made the applications above.

Phase IV: The Creative Imagination
Be with your silence and center your attention.

Visualize each of the first three priorities you have identified from your intuition. Envision yourself choosing each of the options, and describe what the consequences would be. Write these perceptions in your journal.

Apply four questions to the experience of creative imagination.

1. Which course flowed the freest in your imagination?
2. Which excited you the most?
3. Which seemed right for you?
4. Which had the most connection with your personal history?

Phase V: The Use of Memory
Review the three scenarios you have entertained in your creative imagination. What aspects of your life story does each connect with positively? Negatively?

Which of these seems to fulfill the intention of Christ for your life?

Which scenario would fulfill existing themes in your personal history?

Phase VI: Decision

Which choice can you make that seems to be in obedience to Jesus Christ?

With what person or persons can you test this discernment?

By God's grace, what three steps can you take now to begin fulfilling God's dream for your life?

Who is one person you can ask to hold you accountable?

Phase VII: Living Into Your Discernment

After a few months, review the decision if the will of God has not become evident to you.

Be patient, if it has not, and know that sometimes only eternity holds the final answer.

Notes

1. Anthony De Mello, *The Song of the Bird* (Garden City, N.Y.: Doubleday & Co., Image Books, 1984), pp. 22–23.

2. Jolande Jacobi, *The Psychology of C. G. Jung* (New Haven, Conn.: Yale University Press, 1973), p. 107.

3. Erik H. Erikson, *Identity, Youth, and Crisis* (New York: W. W. Norton & Co., 1968), p. 92.

4. Ibid., pp. 92–93.

5. Ibid., p. 139.

6. Jacobi, *Jung,* p. 107.

7. Adapted from De Mello, *Song,* p. 88.

8. George Bernard Shaw, *Complete Plays with Prefaces,* vol. 2 (New York: Dodd, Mead & Co., 1963), pp. 265–429.

9. Frederick Buechner, *A Room Called Remember* (San Francisco: Harper & Row, 1984), p. 4.

10. Carlo Carretto, *The God Who Comes* (Maryknoll, N.Y.: Orbis Books, 1974), p. 39.

11. N. Richard Nash, *The Rainmaker* (New York: Bantam Books, 1957), p. 99.

12. Shaw, *Plays,* pp. vii–clv.